Good Housekeeping

NEW · BASIC COOKERY

THE BEST INTRODUCTORY
BOOK FOR THE COOK

Good Housekeeping
NEW · BASIC COOKERY

THE BEST INTRODUCTORY
BOOK FOR THE COOK

Ebury Press
London

First published 1966
Completely revised editions 1991 and 1995

1 3 5 7 9 10 8 6 4 2

First published in the United Kingdom in 1995 by Ebury Press, Random House,
20 Vauxhall Bridge Road, London SW1V 2SA

Random House Australia (Pty) Limited
20 Alfred Street, Milsons Point, Sydney
New South Wales 2061, Australia

Random House New Zealand Limited
18 Poland Road, Glenfield
Auckland 10, New Zealand

Random House South Africa (Pty) Limited
PO Box 337, Bergvlei, South Africa

Random House UK Limited Reg. No. 954009

A CIP catalogue record for this book is available from the British Library

ISBN 0 09 180994 0

Typeset by SX Composing, Rayleigh, Essex
Printed and bound in Great Britain by
Mackays of Chatham PLC, Chatham, Kent

CONTENTS

INTRODUCTION

WORKING FROM A RECIPE

Before you start to make a dish, read the recipe right through and read also any general instructions at the beginning of the section or chapter. Next, collect together the cooking utensils you will need and do any preliminary preparation, such as greasing dishes, lining cake tins and so on. If the dish is to be baked, turn on the heat and set the thermostatic control so that the oven will be at the correct temperature when you are ready for it.

Finally, collect and measure out all the ingredients needed. If you are a beginner, it is sensible to follow the recipe exactly, scrupulously weighing and measuring the ingredients – leave variations for when you have more experience. Amounts of flavourings, seasonings and spices, sweetening, etc, may usually be varied to suit individual tastes, but basic ingredients like flour or fat should not be altered.

Follow closely the directions given in the recipe – seemingly slight changes in procedure may make all the difference between an outstanding dish and one that is only mediocre.

USING YOUR OVEN

1. Arrange the oven shelves before the oven is heated.
2. Set the thermostat to the required temperature 15–20 minutes before the food is to be put in. (Some dishes, such as milk puddings and casseroles, which require very long, slow cooking, can 'start from cold'.)
3. The centre of the oven corresponds most exactly to the dial setting; usually the upper part in some ovens is somewhat hotter, while the bottom of the oven is cooler.
4. Open the oven door as little as possible during the cooking time. With cakes in particular be very gentle, as an in-rush of cold air may spoil the baking.
5. When using the oven for browning au gratin dishes, etc, have it very hot and place the dishes at the top, otherwise the mixture will bubble without browning.
6. Put the pie dishes, casseroles, cake tins, etc, on baking sheets so that they are easier to move and so that juices do not bubble all over the oven.
7. If you have a fan assisted oven, read the instruction book and turn down the temperature where suggested.

This table compares oven thermostats marked in °C with those marked in °F and with gas marks. These are dial markings and not exact conversions.

°C	°F	gas mark
290	550	
270	525	
250	500	
240	475	9
230	450	8
220	425	7
200	400	6
190	375	5
180	350	4
170	325	3
150	300	2
140	275	1
130	250	½
110	225	¼
100	200	Low
80	175	
70	150	

MEASUR-ING

Use these equivalents to convert recipes from Imperial to metric measures or *vice versa*.

Imperial measurement	Approx. metric equivalent	Imperial measurement	Approx. metric equivalent
1 oz	25 g	9 oz	250 g
2 oz	50 g	10 oz	275 g
3 oz	75 g	11 oz	300 g
4 oz	100–125 g	12 oz	350 g
5 oz	150 g	13 oz	375 g
6 oz	175 g	14 oz	400 g
7 oz	200 g	15 oz	425 g
8 oz	225 g	16 oz (1 lb)	450 g

Imperial measurement	Approx. metric equivalent	Imperial measurement	Approx. metric equivalent
1 fl oz	25 ml	15 fl oz (¾ pint)	450 ml
2 fl oz	50 ml	20 fl oz (1 pint)	600 ml
5 fl oz (¼ pint)	150 ml	35 fl oz	1 litre
10 fl oz (½ pint)	300 ml		

QUICK HANDY MEASURES

Approximate equivalent shown in level 15-ml spoonfuls

Almonds, ground	$25 g = 3\frac{1}{2}$
Breadcrumbs, fresh	$25 g = 7$
Breadcrumbs, dried	$25 g = 3$
Butter, lard, etc	$25 g = 2$
Cheddar, grated	$25 g = 3$
Chocolate, grated	$25 g = 4$
Coffee, instant	$25 g = 6\frac{1}{2}$
Cornflour	$25 g = 2\frac{3}{4}$
Custard powder	$25 g = 2\frac{3}{4}$
Curry powder	$25 g = 4$
Flour, unsifted	$25 g = 3$
Sugar, caster/gran.	$25 g = 2$
Sugar, demerara	$25 g = 2$
Sugar, icing	$25 g = 3$
Syrup or honey	$25 g = 1$

When following a recipe, choose either Imperial or metric measures and do not switch from one to the other. Use standard measuring spoons for small measures.

COOKING EQUIP-MENT

Excellent meals can be produced with surprisingly little equipment, but it does make the work easier if you have the right utensils and a few labour-saving devices that you can really use.

Make your own list of the basic items, using the notes below as a guide but bearing in mind your own circumstances. As storage space and cash allow you can then add other more expensive and specialised items which you would like. Avoid buying odd gadgets unless you are sure they will do a real job for you.

Pots and pans
4 saucepans with lids in assorted sizes
1 milk saucepan, with non-stick finish, for sauces, etc
20.5-cm (8-inch) frying pan of fairly heavy quality (non-stick)
1.7-litre (3-pint) kettle
wok (optional)
steamer (optional)

Kitchen china and ovenware
mixing bowl
2 pudding basins
2 casseroles 1 large, 1 smaller
2 ovenproof plates
coffee pot or percolator

Baking tins
set of bun tins
18-cm (7-inch) cake tin
23-cm (9-inch) cake tin

two 18-cm (7-inch) sandwich tins, 2.5–4 cm (1–1½ inches) deep
Swiss roll tin
18-cm (7-inch) pie plate
baking sheet
wire cooling rack
roasting tin

Other utensils and equipment
kitchen scales
chopping boards
rolling pin
pastry brush
grater with 2 or 3 sizes of hole
electric whisk and/or rotary egg whisk
food processor and/or electric blender
lemon squeezer
colander
sieve
can opener
measuring jug
measuring spoons
set of pastry cutters
2 wooden spoons
2 forks
2 tablespoons
2 teaspoons
slotted draining spoon
ladle
fish slice
skewers
potato peeler
apple corer
4 knives – 1 chopping, 1 vegetable, 1 bread and 1 carving
carving fork
spatula
potato masher
pair kitchen scissors
corkscrew/bottle opener
grapefruit knife

Storage equipment, etc
vegetable rack
storage jars and containers
bread bin
cake and biscuit tins
preserving jars
pedal bin

GLOSSARY

Bain Marie A vessel half-filled with just simmering water, used to keep sauces and soups hot without further cooking, or to prevent overheating of egg dishes baked in the oven.

Bake To cook in the oven by dry heat. Most cakes, pastries and breads are cooked this way, as well as some puddings and savoury dishes.

Baste To spoon over liquid (stock or fat) during cooking to prevent food drying out and to improve the appearance.

Beat To agitate an ingredient or mixture by vigorously turning it over and over with an upward motion, to incorporate air.

Bind To add a liquid, egg or melted fat to a dry mixture to hold it together.

Blanch To treat food with boiling water in order to whiten it, preserve its natural colour, loosen its skin, remove any strong or bitter taste or kill unwanted enzymes or bacteria before freezing or preserving.

Blend To mix flour, cornflour or similar with a cold liquid to form a smooth paste. A little hot liquid is then added, usually from the sauce, soup or stew to be thickened. This prevents lumps forming.

Boil To cook vegetables, rice, pasta etc in liquid heated to 100°C (212°F). Syrups and glazes that need to be reduced in quantity and thickened are also boiled.

Braise To bake or stew slowly on a bed of vegetables in a covered dish.

Consistency The term used to describe the texture of a cake or pudding mixture before it is cooked.

Pouring consistency: The mixture should be soft enough to pour steadily from the bowl and find its own level.

Coating Consistency: The mixture should be thick enough to coat the back of a spoon.

Dropping Consistency: Fill a spoon with some of the mixture and hold it on its side above the bowl without jerking. The mixture should fall off reluctantly.

Cream To beat together fat and sugar to resemble whipped cream ie until pale and fluffy. This is used for cake and pudding mixtures.

Dice To cut up into small cubes.

Drain To remove surplus liquid or fat from foods by using a slotted spoon, colander, sieve or kitchen spoon.

Dredge, dust or flour To sprinkle food lightly with flour before frying or sugar to improve appearance.

Fold in To combine a whisked or creamed mixture with other ingredients so that it retains its lightness. This method is used for cake mixtures, soufflés and meringues and is done with a metal spoon; it cannot be successfully done in an electric food processor.

Fry To cook food in deep or shallow hot fat.

Glaze To give food a glossy surface before or after cooking. It improves flavour and appearance.

Grill To cook food in direct heat under a grill.

Knead To work a dough firmly using the heel of the hand for breadmaking, the fingertips in pastry making. In both cases the outside of the dough is drawn to the centre.

Poach To cook gently in liquid just below boiling point.

Purée To pass vegetables or fruit through a sieve to remove skins, fibres and pips and give a smooth, even texture. This can also be done in an electric blender or food processor.

Roast To cook meat or poultry in hot fat in the oven. Potatoes and vegetables may also be cooked in this way.

Roux A mixture of equal quantities of fat and flour cooked together for a few minutes. The mixture is used as a foundation for sauces.

Rubbing in A method of incorporating fat into flour, used in making shortcrust pastry, plain cakes and biscuits, when a short texture is required. The fat is cut into small pieces in the flour, then rubbed in with the fingertips.

Sauté To cook over a brisk heat in a fat such as butter or oil. The food must be tossed in the fat, either by shaking the pan or turning with a spatula so that it does not stick or burn.

Sieve To rub or press food through a sieve using a wooden spoon.

Sift To shake flour or similar through a sieve to aerate.

Simmer To keep a cooking liquid just below boiling point. The surface of the liquid should bubble very gently.

Steam To cook food in the steam from boiling water.

Stew To cook slowly and for a long time in an enclosed vessel.

Whisk or whip To beat air rapidly into a mixture either by hand using an egg beater, balloon whisk or electric mixer. It is continued until the food is quite stiff.

BREAKFASTS

Weekday breakfasts tend to become a hurried, skimped affair of a piece of toast and a quick cup of tea — the old-fashioned hearty breakfast is now a weekend or holiday treat. However, it is important to start the day with an adequate even if light meal. Many people find cereal or fruit, followed by toast and marmalade, are quite sufficient, but some require a more substantial breakfast with something cooked. Any cooked dish for breakfast use needs to be quickly prepared, so frying, poaching and grilling are the most popular methods to use. Try to keep frying to a minimum for health reasons. To save time in the morning, it is a good plan to lay the table the night before and to leave ready everything that will be needed for the meal.

BREAK-FAST FRUITS

Almost any fresh or stewed fruit is suitable for eating at breakfast, either alone or mixed with cereals; it is usually served simply in individual dishes. If necessary, some fresh fruit, such as oranges and grapefruit, may be prepared overnight, though as this results in the loss of the valuable vitamin C, it should not be done as a general rule. Don't prepare fruits such as apples, pears or bananas in advance as they will discolour.

Fruit juices are another popular breakfast item; prepare your own fresh juice if you wish, but cartoned, bottled, canned or frozen products are easier and cheaper to use and nutritionally just as sound. Serve them either neat or diluted with water. The most usual breakfast juices are unsweetened grapefruit and orange, but the juice of other fruits, such as blackcurrants or raspberries, may be served when in season.

> To obtain the juice from soft fruit, simmer it gently with a little water until tender; strain or sieve and sweeten if necessary.

ORANGES

Peel the oranges, removing as much as possible of the white pith, then slice fairly thinly across the segments. Flick out any pips with the point of a knife. Sprinkle with sugar if you wish.

GRAPEFRUIT

Cut the fruit in half and cut round each half with a curved grapefruit knife, loosening the flesh from the outer skin. Cut between the segments to loosen the flesh from the membranes, remove the centre core and pips. Sprinkle with sugar if you wish.

CEREALS

PREPARED CEREALS

There are many popular ready-to-serve cereals on the market, which require no preparation at all. They may be served with hot or cold milk, natural yogurt and sugar if not already sweetened, or with fruit — fresh, canned or stewed.

MUESLI

Makes 14 servings

250 g (9 oz) porridge oats
75 g (3 oz) wholewheat
   flakes
50 g (2 oz) bran buds
75 g (3 oz) sunflower seeds

175 g (6 oz) sultanas
175 g (6 oz) dried pears
   (or apricots, figs or
   peaches), cut into small
   pieces

Mix together the porridge oats, wholewheat flakes, bran buds, sunflower seeds, sultanas and dried pears. (The dried fruits can be varied according to taste and availability, but keep the ratio of grains to fruit about the same.) ■ The dry muesli will keep fresh for several weeks if stored in an airtight container.

APPLE MUESLI

Serves 4

60 ml (4 level tbsp) rolled
   oats or fine oatmeal
150 ml (¼ pint) fruit juice
4 eating apples
60 ml (4 tbsp) cream

15 ml (1 tbsp) honey
a little brown sugar
50 g (2 oz) sultanas or
   raisins
a few chopped nuts
   (walnuts, almonds, etc)

Place the oats and fruit juice in a bowl and leave overnight ■ The next day grate the apples (with their skins on); keep a little back for decoration and mix the rest with the remaining ingredients (except the nuts) ■ Put into glasses, top with some grated apple and sprinkle with chopped nuts.

YOGURT WITH DRIED FRUIT

Serves 4

350 g (12 oz) dried fruit
   (see below)
about 50 g (2 oz)
   demerara sugar

piece of lemon rind
plain yogurt to serve

Choose from the wide range of dried fruits — apricots, prunes, figs, pears, apples or peaches. Serve just one fruit or make a dried fruit salad. Wash the fruit and soak it for several hours (or overnight) in 600 ml (1 pint) water. Cook it in this water, adding the sugar and lemon rind. Stew gently till tender and serve cold with plain yogurt.

PORRIDGE

Serves 2–3

600 ml (1 pint) water or milk and water mixed

50 g (2 oz) rolled oats
salt to taste

Heat the water and when it is boiling sprinkle in the oats, stirring vigorously with a wooden spoon. Continue to stir and boil for about 5 minutes, then add salt to taste; serve very hot.

EGGS

Eggs can be quickly cooked in a variety of ways for breakfast, but because they are relatively high in cholesterol nutritionists recommend that we eat no more than about 3 per week.
Raw or lightly cooked eggs can sometimes be a source of food poisoning (see overleaf) and should be avoided by 'at risk' groups.

HOW TO BREAK AN EGG
Hold the egg over the saucepan or a bowl, and either gently tap it on the side of the pan or bowl, or give it a gentle tap with a knife to break the shell. Put your thumbs on each side of the crack and pull the shell apart ■ To separate the yolk from the white, tip the yolk carefully from one half of the shell to the other, until all the white has slid into the bowl below.

BOILED EGGS

1–2 eggs per person

Lower the eggs gently into a pan of boiling water, using a spoon. Lower the heat and cook for $3\frac{1}{2}$ minutes for a light set, and up to 5 minutes for a firmer set ■ Alternatively, put them in cold water and bring slowly to the boil – then cook for 3–4 minutes ■ Fresh eggs take a little longer to cook than those which are a few days old.

POACHED EGGS

1–2 eggs per person
butter

salt and pepper
buttered toast to serve

Melting butter in each cup

Simmer some water gently in the lower pan of the poacher and melt a small knob of butter in each cup ■ Break the eggs one at a time and put into the cups; season lightly, cover and simmer gently for 3–4 minutes, or until lightly set ■ Serve on hot buttered toast ■ To poach eggs in a frying pan, half fill it with water and add a pinch of salt or a few drops of vinegar ■ Bring the water to the boil and slip the eggs into the water. Cook gently until lightly set and lift out with a slotted spoon or fish slice ■ Drain the eggs before serving.

FRIED EGGS

lard, oil or dripping   1–2 eggs per person

Heat the fat in a frying pan. Break each egg into a cup, drop carefully into the hot fat and cook gently until set, basting with hot fat so that the eggs are cooked on top ▪ Remove from the pan with a fish slice or spatula.

SCRAMBLED EGGS

Serves 2

25 g (1 oz) butter or
  margarine
4 eggs

60 ml (4 tbsp) milk
salt and pepper
buttered toast to serve

Melt the butter or margarine slowly in a saucepan ▪ Break 4 eggs one at a time into a basin, add the milk and some seasoning ▪ Pour the egg mixture into the pan, cook slowly over gentle heat, stirring all the time until the mixture is creamy ▪ Serve on hot buttered toast.

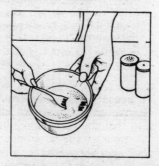

Mixing egg and milk

Eggs can sometimes be a source of salmonella, one of the bacteria responsible for causing food poisoning. Raw or lightly cooked eggs are a potential risk because they will not have been cooked sufficiently to kill any salmonella which may be present. Although the chance of an egg being contaminated is minimal, it is important for those who are particularly vulnerable to avoid eating raw or lightly cooked eggs. 'At risk' groups are infants under 2, pregnant women, the elderly, and anyone who is already ill or has an impaired immune system.

SAUSAGES

Both pork and beef sausages may be used for breakfast, either grilled or fried; they can be served with fried bread, tomatoes or mushrooms. Sausagemeat may be made into flat cakes, which are fried or baked.

GRILLED SAUSAGES

Serves 4

450 g (1 lb) pork or beef
  sausages

Cook under a fairly hot grill, turning frequently until evenly browned and cooked through; allow about 15–20 minutes.

FRIED SAUSAGES

Serves 4

450 g (1 lb) pork or beef sausages   25 g (1 oz) fat

Heat the fat in a frying pan, then add the sausages carefully and cook them gently, browning them evenly ▪ It is important to cook slowly, so that the skins do not split and so that the insides are thoroughly done. Allow about 15–20 minutes, according to size.

BACON

Bacon, either fried or grilled, and served with a fried egg and fried bread, is probably the favourite English breakfast dish.

> When buying bacon remember that the fat should be firm and white and the lean a deep pink. Back, streaky, collar or gammon rashers are all suitable for both frying and grilling. Bacon is usually sliced rather thinly, but gammon is generally preferred cut a little thicker.

To prepare bacon for cooking, cut off the rind and remove any bones with kitchen scissors. To make sure that the rashers will be quite flat when cooked, snip through the fat at intervals. If on the other hand you like a wavy effect in the cooked rashers, smooth them with the flat of a knife. Unless the bacon is very lean, no extra fat is needed.

GRILLED BACON

bacon rashers   fat or oil

Lay the rashers on the grill rack with the fat parts overlapping the lean. Place under a hot grill, turning them once ▪ Lean rashers should be brushed with fat or oil before cooking ▪ Cook quickly for crisp bacon, slowly if you prefer the rashers softer.

FRIED BACON

bacon rashers – allow 1–2 per person

Lay streaky or back rasher in a cold pan, with the lean parts overlapping the fat. Cook very gently, especially at first while the fat is melting ▪ Turn once during cooking.

FRIED BREAD

For this traditional accompaniment to the cooked British breakfast, heat some fat in a frying pan and fry the slices of bread until crisp on both sides.

KIPPERS

Kippered herrings may be purchased boned or unboned, wrapped or unwrapped, frozen or fresh. When serving whole kippers, allow 1–2 per person, according to size. Prepare by washing in cold water, then cutting off the heads, small fins and tail, using kitchen scissors.

POACHED KIPPERS

1–2 whole kippers or   butter
   3–4 fillets per person

Put the fish into a frying pan, cover with boiling water and poach gently for about 5 minutes or until tender. Drain and serve with a knob of butter on each kipper.

> To reduce the rather unpleasant smell from kippers, they may be cooked in a covered dish: pour on boiling water and cover closely with a lid or plate. Leave for 5–10 minutes, pour off the water and serve with a knob of butter.

Covering the kippers with water

GRILLED KIPPERS

1–2 whole kippers or   butter
   3–4 fillets per person

Dot the kippers with butter and grill gently for 4–5 minutes on each side.

BAKED KIPPERS

1–2 whole kippers or   butter
   3–4 fillets per person

Wrap the kippers in foil and place in the oven at 190°C (375°F) mark 5. Serve with a knob of butter.

KIDNEYS

Lamb's and calf's kidneys have a better flavour and are much more acceptable for breakfast than ox or pig's kidneys. Served with bacon, they make a good substantial breakfast. Allow 1½–2 kidneys per person. For Grilled Kidneys see recipe on page 54. For Fried Kidneys, prepare as for Grilled Kidneys but dip the kidneys in a little seasoned flour and fry in hot fat for 10 minutes.

COFFEE

COFFEE

There are many different types of coffee available each with its distinctive flavour. It is worth trying a few separately and in a blend until you find the ones you like ■ There are also different grades of roasted beans, the degree of roasting affecting the flavour of the coffee, dark beans (high-roasted) giving a stronger flavour ■ You can buy roasted beans and grind them yourself, or you can buy vacuum-packed ready-ground coffee. It is essential to choose the correct grind for your method of making coffee.

Good coffee may be made in several ways and it is not essential to have special equipment. Whichever method is followed, however, you must use fresh coffee and sufficient of it. For breakfast it is usual to serve coffee with hot milk – generally 1 part milk to 2 parts coffee. The milk should be hot, but never boiled, and is served in a separate heated jug. Black coffee is usually made quite strong.

All the equipment must be kept scrupulously clean or the coffee will be unsatisfactory. If it is necessary to reheat coffee, do not let it boil.

Making coffee in an earthenware jug

Find out the approximate capacity of your jug so that you can judge the amount of water in it. Warm the jug, then put in 40–50 g (1½–2 oz) medium-ground coffee per 600 ml (1 pint) water. Pour on fast-boiling water, stir vigorously, cover and keep in a warm place to infuse for 4–5 minutes. Strain the coffee into a warmed coffee pot or straight into the cups.

Straining the coffee into pot

Making coffee in a saucepan

Put the measured water in a saucepan with 40–50 g (1½–2 oz) medium or coarsely-ground coffee per 600 ml (1 pint) and place over the heat. Stir well and bring almost to boiling point. Remove the pan from the heat, stir, cover the pan and leave in a warm place or over a very low heat for about 5 minutes. Strain the coffee into a heated jug.

Instant coffee

Allow 5 ml (1 level tsp) instant powder or granules per cup. Fill the cups three-quarters full with boiling water and top up with warm or cold milk, if liked.

Making coffee in a percolator

Place 40–50 g (1½–2 oz) medium or coarsely-ground coffee per 600 ml (1 pint) water in the perforated basket and put the water in the base. Bring the water to the boil, lower the heat and allow the water to percolate through the coffee for 8–10 minutes. Remove coffee basket and serve at once.

Placing coffee in basket

Using a cona or syphon machine

Place the water in the lower bowl and put on to heat. Place the filter in the neck of the upper bowl and put in 40–50 g (1½–2 oz) medium-ground coffee per 600 ml (1 pint) water. When the water in the lower bowl boils, fit the upper bowl on top. Allow the water to rise to the upper bowl. Leave to infuse for 2–3 minutes, then draw the machine from the heat and allow the water to run back into the lower bowl.

Placing coffee in upper bowl

Using a cafetière

A cafetière is a heatproof glass jug with a fine wire mesh plunger which is used to push coffee grounds to the bottom of the jug. Allow 40–50 g (1½–2 oz) medium-ground coffee per 600 ml (1 pint) boiling water.

Filter coffee

Place a filter paper in the filter attachment and put in 75 ml (5 level tbsp) finely-ground coffee per 600 ml (1 pint) water. Place the filter over a heated jug and pour boiling water slowly over the coffee grounds, allowing it to filter through. Electric coffee makers boil the water, syphon it over the grounds and keep the coffee hot for you.

Placing coffee in filter

TEA

Buy tea in small quantities and keep it in an airtight tin or jar so that the aroma and strength are conserved.

The usual amount to allow is 5 ml (1 level tsp) per person; when making tea for more than three people, it is usual to allow 5 ml (1 level tsp) per person and 5 ml (1 level tsp) 'for the pot'. Use freshly boiled water.

Warm the pot, put in the measured quantity of tea, pour on the boiling water and leave to infuse before pouring out. The time required for infusion depends on the type of tea used; Indian teas usually require 4–5 minutes, but China teas infuse more quickly and can be poured out 2–3 minutes after being made.

When using teabags allow 1 bag per person (don't add an extra one 'for the pot').

Indian teas are usually taken with milk, with or without sugar to taste, but some people prefer sliced lemon to milk. China teas are always served with lemon slices, not milk.

Pouring on the boiling water

SOUPS AND STARTERS

STOCKS

Good full-bodied stock is the foundation of great soups and casseroles. When possible make your own, but there are numerous ready-made stock preparations – the most popular being stock cubes – which save much time and trouble. Don't forget that these are well seasoned and inclined to be salty – so do not add extra seasoning until after checking the flavour at the final stage. If you have a freezer, keep stock frozen for up to 3 months as a useful standby.

BASIC MEAT STOCK

Makes about
1.1 litres (2 pints)

900 g (2 lb) meat bones, fresh or from cooked meat
2 litres (3½ pints) water
2 onions, skinned and roughly chopped
2 sticks celery, scrubbed and roughly chopped
2 carrots, peeled and roughly chopped
5 ml (1 level tsp) salt
3 peppercorns
a bouquet garni

Wash the bones and chop them up. Put them in a large saucepan and add 2 litres (3½ pints) water; bring to the boil and skim off any scum ■ Add the roughly chopped vegetables, salt, peppercorns and bouquet garni and simmer, tightly covered, for 3 hours ■ If you have a pressure cooker, use only 1.4 litres (2½ pints) water, bring to high pressure and cook for 1–1¼ hours. Reduce pressure at room temperature ■ When cooked, strain the stock and leave to go cold. Chill and remove all traces of fat.

CHICKEN STOCK

Makes about
1.1 litres (2 pints)

roast chicken carcass
flavouring vegetables (onions, carrots, celery)
herbs
1.4–1.7 litres (2½–3 pints) water

Break down the carcass and bones of a carved roast chicken and include any skin, chicken scraps, etc. Add the water and bring to the boil ■ Skim off any scum that rises and add flavouring vegetables and herbs if you wish. Cover tightly and simmer for 3 hours ■ If you have a pressure cooker, use only 1.1 litres (2 pints) water, bring to high pressure and cook for 45–60 minutes. Reduce pressure at room temperature ■ When cooked, strain the stock and leave to go cold. Chill and remove all traces of fat.

FRENCH ONION SOUP

Serves 4

40 g (1½ oz) butter or margarine
225 g (8 oz) onions, skinned and chopped
15 ml (1 level tbsp) plain flour

900 ml (1½ pints) beef stock
salt and pepper
a bay leaf
4 slices French bread
grated cheese

Melt the butter and fry the onions until they are well and evenly browned, taking care not to let them become too dark. Add the flour and mix well ∎ Pour on the boiling stock, add some salt and pepper and the bay leaf and simmer for 30 minutes; remove the bay leaf ∎ Put the slices of French bread in a soup tureen, pour on the soup and top with grated cheese ∎ Alternatively, pour the soup into a fire-proof casserole, float the slices of bread on it and cover with the grated cheese; then brown under the grill for a few minutes.

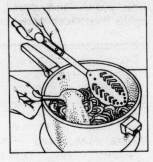

Adding the flour

TOMATO SOUP

Serves 4

25 g (1 oz) butter or margarine
1 stick of celery, washed and chopped
1 small onion, skinned and finely chopped
1 carrot, peeled and sliced
1 rasher of bacon, rinded and chopped
30 ml (2 level tbsp) plain flour

a bouquet garni
700 g (1½ lb) tomatoes, quartered
600 ml (1 pint) chicken stock
salt and pepper
a little sugar
lemon juice

Melt the butter and cook the celery, onion, carrot and bacon for 5 minutes. Sprinkle in the flour and stir well ∎ Add the bouquet garni, tomatoes, stock and seasoning. Cover and cook gently for 30 minutes ∎ Rub the soup through a sieve or purée it in a blender then sieve to remove the seeds and any small pieces of skin. Return it to the pan, check the seasoning, add a little sugar and lemon juice and reheat.

CREAM OF MUSHROOM SOUP

Serves 4

225 g (8 oz) mushrooms, sliced
1 small onion, skinned and sliced
300 ml (½ pint) chicken stock
25 g (1 oz) butter or margarine
45 ml (3 level tbsp) plain flour
450 ml (¾ pint) milk
salt and pepper
45 ml (3 tbsp) cream

Cook the mushrooms and onion in the stock, covered, for about 30 minutes. Let them cool slightly then purée in a blender or rub through a sieve ■ Melt the butter, stir in the flour and cook for 2–3 minutes. Remove the pan from the heat and gradually stir in the milk; bring to the boil and continue to stir until it thickens ■ Add the mushroom purée, season with salt and pepper and simmer for 15 minutes. Allow to cool slightly and stir in the cream ■ Reheat without boiling and, if you wish, garnish with lightly fried sliced mushrooms.

> Soup is often served accompanied by croûtons, little pieces of bread which are fried or toasted, and sprinkled over the soup.

MINESTRONE

Serves 4

½ leek, shredded and washed
1 onion, skinned and finely chopped
1 garlic clove, skinned and crushed
25 g (1 oz) butter or margarine
1 litre (1¾ pints) beef stock
1 carrot, peeled and cut in thin strips
1 turnip, peeled and cut in thin strips
1 stick of celery, trimmed and thinly sliced
45 ml (3 level tbsp) shortcut macaroni
¼ cabbage, washed and finely shredded
3 runner beans, thinly sliced
45 ml (3 tbsp) fresh or frozen peas
5 ml (1 level tsp) tomato purée or 4 tomatoes, skinned and diced
1–2 rashers of bacon, rinded, chopped and fried
salt and pepper
grated Parmesan cheese

Rinding bacon

Lightly fry the leek, onion and garlic in the melted butter for 5–10 minutes, until soft ■ Add the stock, bring to the boil, add the carrot, turnip, celery and macaroni and simmer, covered, for 20–30 minutes ■ Add the cabbage, beans and peas, cover and simmer for a further 20 minutes ■ Stir in the tomato purée or tomatoes, bacon and seasoning to taste. Bring back to the boil. Serve the grated Parmesan cheese in a separate dish.

WATERCRESS SOUP

Serves 4

2 bunches watercress
50 g (2 oz) butter or margarine
1 onion, skinned and chopped
25 g (1 oz) plain flour
750 ml (1¼ pints) chicken stock
300 ml (½ pint) milk
salt and pepper

Wash the watercress and reserve a few sprigs to garnish. Cut away any coarse stalks. Chop the leaves and remaining stalks ▪ Melt the butter in a pan and stir in the watercress and onion. Cook over a gentle heat for about 15 minutes until soft. Stir in the flour, then the stock, milk and seasoning. Bring to the boil, stirring continuously. Simmer gently for 30 minutes ▪ Cool slightly, then purée in a blender or rub through a sieve ▪ Return the soup to the pan and reheat. Garnish with watercress.

CHICKEN SOUP

Serves 4

25 g (1 oz) butter or margarine
1 medium onion, skinned and finely chopped
30 ml (2 level tbsp) plain flour
600 ml (1 pint) chicken stock
about 100 g (4 oz) cold cooked chicken
300 ml (½ pint) milk
1.25 ml (¼ level tsp) ground nutmeg
1.25 ml (¼ level tsp) dried thyme
salt and pepper
45 ml (3 tbsp) single cream
chopped fresh parsley to serve

Melt the butter in a large saucepan and fry the onion gently for 5 minutes until soft ▪ Stir in the flour then, stirring all the time, add the chicken stock, chicken, milk, nutmeg, thyme, and salt and pepper to taste. Bring to the boil then cover and simmer gently for 5 minutes ▪ Stir in the cream and serve sprinkled with chopped parsley.

CHICKEN LIVER PÂTÉ

Serves 8

700 g (1½ lb) chicken livers
75 g (3 oz) butter
1 medium onion, skinned and finely chopped
1 large garlic clove, skinned and crushed
15 ml (1 tbsp) double cream
30 ml (2 level tbsp) tomato purée
45 ml (3 tbsp) sherry or brandy
melted butter (optional)

Rinse the chicken livers and dry thoroughly on absorbent kitchen paper ▪ Fry them in the butter until they change colour. Reduce the heat, add the onion and garlic, cover and cook for 5 minutes. Remove from the heat and cool ▪ Add the cream, tomato purée and sherry or brandy. Purée in a blender or press through a sieve ▪ Turn into 8 individual dishes and cover the tops with melted butter if you wish. Chill.

MACKEREL PÂTÉ

Serves 4

350 g (12 oz) smoked
  mackerel fillets
50 g (2 oz) butter,
  softened
60 ml (4 level tbsp)
  mayonnaise
5 ml (1 level tsp) snipped
  fresh chives

freshly ground pepper
grated rind and juice of
  ½ a lemon
parsley sprigs and lemon
  slices to garnish
fingers of hot toast to
  serve

Remove the skin and any bones from the mackerel fillets ■ Place the flesh in a bowl and add the butter, mayonnaise, chives, pepper, lemon rind and juice. Mix well together ■ Divide the pâté equally between 4 individual dishes and garnish with parsley and lemon slices ■ Serve with fingers of hot toast.

Removing skin

DRESSED AVOCADOS

ripe avocados (allow half
  per person)
lemon juice
French dressing (see page
  68), or

shelled prawns plus thin
  mayonnaise (see page
  68) or soured cream
  and seasoning
lettuce leaves (optional)

Removing stone

Cut open the avocados lengthwise, using a stainless steel knife and making a deep cut through the flesh, up to the stone and entirely encircling the fruit ■ Separate the halves by gently rotating them in opposite directions and discard the stone. Brush the cut surfaces with lemon juice ■ Serve with French dressing spooned into the hollow of each avocado half, or fill the hollow with shelled prawns moistened with thin mayonnaise or well-seasoned soured cream. If you wish serve the avocados on lettuce leaves ■ A ripe avocado 'gives' slightly when pressed at the pointed end.

CORN ON THE COB

corn cobs (allow 1–2 per
  person)

salt and pepper
melted butter

Remove the sheath and silky threads from the corn ■ Cook in boiling unsalted water for 12–20 minutes, or until the kernels are soft ■ Sprinkle with salt and pepper and serve with melted butter; put a cocktail stick in each end of the cobs to make them easier to eat.

Removing sheath and threads

Salt added to the water will toughen the corn, so do not add it until serving.

FLORIDA COCKTAIL

Serves 4

2 small grapefruit
2 large oranges
sugar

curaçao or any orange liqueur (optional)

Working over a plate, prepare the grapefruit as follows: remove all the skin, peeling the fruit with a sawing action and cutting deep enough to show the pulp ■ Holding the fruit in one hand, remove the flesh of each segment by cutting down at the side of the membrane and then scraping the segment off the membrane on the opposite side on to the plate ■ Repeat the process for the oranges. Mix the segments, together with any juice collected on the plate. Add curaçao if you wish and sugar, to taste ■ Divide the fruit between 4 glasses and pour a little juice into each. Serve chilled.

BLUE CHEESE DIP

100 g (4 oz) Danish Blue or Roquefort cheese, softened
75 g (3 oz) full fat soft cheese, softened

15 ml (1 tbsp) lemon juice
salt

Blend all the ingredients to a smooth cream with salt to taste and serve with chunks of French bread or vegetable dunks such as carrot sticks, radishes, celery curls, cucumber sticks.

FISH

TYPES OF FISH

Many fish are available frozen. Use like fresh fish but follow any instructions on the pack concerning storage, thawing and cooking.

There are many types of fish sold, but those described here tend to be the most popular in Great Britain.

Cod   A large, white-fleshed fish, which can be bought as fillets, steaks and cutlets. Cod can be grilled, fried or baked or used in made-up dishes. As its taste is not strong, it needs careful seasoning and flavouring.

Coley (Saithe, Coalfish)   A round fish with almost black skin and greyish flesh which turns white on cooking. Use in the same ways as cod or haddock.

Haddock   Another large, white-fleshed fish, with a good flavour. Haddock can be bought as fillets, steaks and cutlets and cooked by most methods.

Finnan haddock   Fairly small haddock, split open and lightly brined, then smoked on the bone. It has an excellent flavour and is traditionally served poached or grilled. When cooked and flaked, it can be used in made-up dishes such as kedgeree.
Golden fillets (or cutlets) have the backbone removed before they are smoked.
Smoked haddock or cod fillets are generally taken from larger fish and may therefore be coarse-textured.

Hake   Similar to cod, but with firmer white flesh. It can be cooked by any method suitable for cod.

Halibut   A large flat fish, usually sold in slices or steaks. It has white flesh and a delicate flavour and is one of the more expensive kinds of fish. It is usually grilled, baked or poached.

FISH

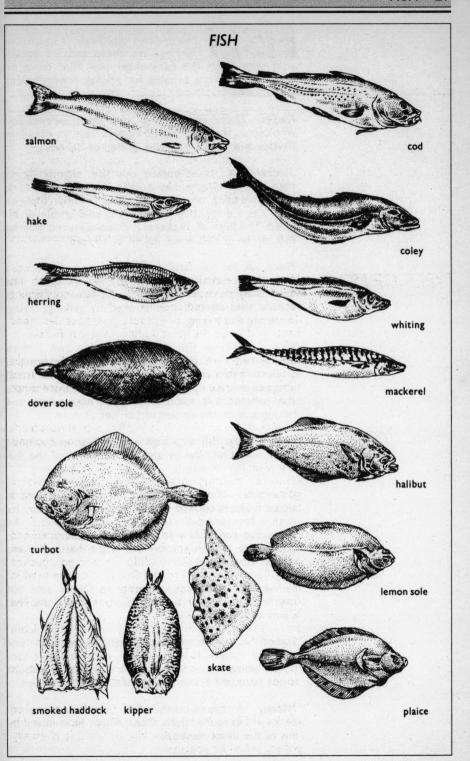

salmon

cod

hake

coley

herring

whiting

dover sole

mackerel

turbot

halibut

lemon sole

smoked haddock   kipper

skate

plaice

Herring   A fairly small, round-bodied fish with a silvery skin and creamy-fawn oily flesh. It has a distinctive flavour. Herrings are cheap and are usually sold whole but the fishmonger will fillet them on request. They are suitable for grilling, frying, baking and sousing.

Kipper   These are herrings split open, brined and smoked on the bone. Good kippers have an excellent flavour and can be poached, grilled or baked.

Mackerel   A round-bodied oily fish, slightly larger than the herring; it has a characteristic green and black marbling on the skin. The creamy-coloured flesh has a distinctive flavour. It is sold whole or filleted. The flesh of mackerel is close-textured and the fish can be grilled, fried, baked or soused.

Plaice   A flat fish with a dark grey top skin dotted with characteristic closely-set orange-red spots. The flesh is white, with a very delicate flavour. Plaice is usually sold filleted; it is cooked by grilling, frying, steaming and baking.

Salmon   A large fish with silvery skin and a deep orange-red flesh that has a firm, close texture and distinctive flavour. Salmon is sold in steaks and as tail end and middle cut pieces; when small, the fish are sold whole. It is suitable for poaching, grilling and baking and can be served either hot or cold.

Skate   A flat fish with slightly pink flesh and a moist shiny skin. Only the 'wings' or side parts of the fish are sold. Fry or poach.

Dover sole   One of the finest flat fish, more oval in shape than plaice, with a darkish brown-grey skin. Its flesh is firm and delicate with a delicious flavour. An expensive fish, it is sold whole or as fillets. Can be cooked by most methods, and is the basis of many classic fish dishes.

Lemon sole (Witch sole)   Similar to Dover sole but the flesh is coarser and the flavour is not so fine. Cook as for plaice.

Turbot   A very large flat fish usually sold in thick slices or cutlets. It is a delicious and expensive fish, but its white flesh is firm in texture, so a large amount is not required. It can be poached, baked or grilled.

Whiting   A round-bodied fish with fine-textured, delicately flavoured flesh. Cook whole or in fillets, by any of the usual methods.

FRIED PLAICE FILLETS

Serves 2

4 fillets of plaice or sole,
 about 175 g (6 oz) per
 person
seasoned flour

1 egg, beaten
dry white breadcrumbs
50 g (2 oz) butter or oil
lemon wedges

Wipe the fillets and dip in seasoned flour, shaking off any excess. Dip the fillets in beaten egg then coat in breadcrumbs, making sure that the coating is firm ■ Fry the fillets in the hot butter or oil for 3–5 minutes; turn them and fry for a further 2–3 minutes until crisp and golden brown ■ Drain on absorbent kitchen paper and serve garnished with lemon wedges.

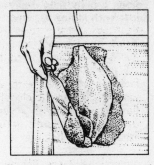

Coating with breadcrumbs

SEASONED FLOUR

Mix about 30 ml (2 level tbsp) flour with about 5 ml (1 level tsp) salt and a good sprinkling of pepper ■ This is used for dusting meat or fish before frying or stewing. Either pat it on to the meat or fish, or dip pieces in the flour and shake them gently before cooking.

BAKED PLAICE WITH MUSHROOMS

Serves 4

8 fillets of plaice
 preferably skinned
a squeeze of lemon juice
salt and pepper
50 g (2 oz) mushrooms,
 sliced

1 small onion, skinned
 and finely chopped
45 ml (3 tbsp) milk
15 ml (1 level tbsp)
 cornflour
sprigs of parsley

Grease an ovenproof dish. Fold each fillet with both ends underneath and place in the dish; squeeze some lemon juice over and season with salt and pepper ■ Sprinkle the mushrooms and onion on top and add the milk. Bake in the oven at 190°C (375°F) mark 5 for 15–20 minutes or until the fish begins to flake apart. Transfer the fillets to a serving dish ■ Blend the cornflour with the remaining fish liquor and put in a saucepan; bring to the boil, stirring constantly, and cook, stirring, for 1 minute. Pour this sauce over the fillets and garnish with parsley.

FISH IN BATTER

Serves 4

oil for deep frying
4 pieces of cod fillet
   (or other fish)
seasoned flour
1 egg
125 g (4 oz) plain flour
150 ml (¼ pint) milk
lemon wedges

Heat the oil slowly in a deep saucepan or deep fat fryer to 177°–188°C (350°–370°F). Wipe the fish and toss in seasoned flour ■ Mix together the egg, flour and half the milk, beat until smooth, then gradually add the rest of the milk, beating all the time ■ Coat the fish with the batter and gently lower it into the fat with a slotted spoon or fish slice. Fry until golden brown, then drain on absorbent kitchen paper. Serve with lemon wedges.

Coating fish with flour   Coating fish with batter

Either use a thermometer to check the correct temperature for frying, or drop a 2.5-cm (1-inch) cube of bread into the hot oil; it should brown in 60 seconds if the oil is ready.

GRILLED MACKEREL

Serves 4

4 mackerel   oil

Wash the mackerel, scrape off the scales and cut off the heads and tails. Slit the underside of the fish and remove the entrails, then wash and dry the fish ■ Make deep slashes in the skin at 3-cm (1¼-inch) intervals and brush with oil ■ Place the mackerel on the grill rack and cook under a hot grill for 5–8 minutes each side, depending on the thickness.

Slashing mackerel

HERRINGS IN OATMEAL

Serves 4

4 herrings, cleaned and
  filleted
salt and pepper

fine oatmeal
50 g (2 oz) lard or butter

Wipe the herrings. Season and coat with oatmeal and fry in hot lard or butter until golden brown, turning once to ensure that they are evenly cooked – about 6–8 minutes. Drain on kitchen paper.

POACHED SMOKED HADDOCK

Serves 4

350–450 g (³/₄–1 lb)
  smoked haddock

butter to serve

Wash the fish and cut off the tail and any fins; if it is large, cut into pieces. Place in a pan, just cover with a little milk and water and cook very gently for 10–15 minutes. Drain and serve with a knob of butter.

FISH PIE

Serves 4

450 g (1 lb) haddock, cod
  or coley fillets
375 ml (13 fl oz) milk
1 bay leaf
6 black peppercorns
onion slices for flavouring
salt and pepper
65 g (2¹/₂ oz) butter or
  margarine
45 ml (3 level tbsp) flour

150 ml (5 fl oz) single
  cream
2 eggs, hard-boiled,
  shelled and chopped
30 ml (2 tbsp) chopped
  fresh parsley
900 g (2 lb) potatoes,
  cooked and mashed
1 egg, beaten, to glaze

Put the fish in a frying pan, pour over 300 ml (¹/₂ pint) milk and add the bay leaf, peppercorns, onion slices and a good pinch of salt. Bring slowly to the boil, cover and simmer for 8–10 minutes, until the fish flakes when tested with a fork ■ Lift the fish out using a fish slice and place on a plate. Flake the fish, discarding skin and bone. Strain and reserve the milk ■ Melt 40 g (1¹/₂ oz) butter in a saucepan, stir in the flour and cook gently for 1 minute, stirring. Remove the pan from the heat and gradually stir in the reserved milk. Bring to the boil slowly and continue to cook, stirring until the sauce thickens. Season ■ Stir in the cream and fish with any juices. Add the chopped egg and parsley and season. Spoon the mixture into a 1.1 litre (2 pint) pie dish or similar ovenproof dish ■ Heat the remaining 75 ml (5 tbsp) milk and 25 g (1 oz) butter in a saucepan then beat into the potato. Season and leave to cool slightly ■ Spoon the cooled potato on top of the fish mixture and roughen the surface with a fork ■ Place the dish on a baking sheet and cook at 200°C (400°F) mark 6 for 10–15 minutes or until the potato is set ■ Beat the egg with a pinch of salt then brush over the pie. Return to the oven for about 15 minutes, until golden brown.

KEDGEREE

Serves 4

350 g (12 oz) cooked
   smoked haddock
2 eggs, hard-boiled
75 g (3 oz) butter or
   margarine

125 g (4 oz) long grain
   rice, cooked
salt and pepper
chopped fresh parsley

Flaking fish with fork

Remove the skin and bone from the haddock and flake the fish with a fork. Chop one of the hard-boiled eggs and mix with the fish ■ Melt the butter in a saucepan and add the rice, fish and egg mixture and seasoning to taste ■ Stir thoroughly over the heat until the kedgeree is heated through, pile it into a serving dish and garnish with chopped parsley and the remaining egg, cut into neat slices.

CHEESY GRILLED COD

Serves 4

4 cod cutlets, weighing
   about 700 g (1½ lb)
100 g (4 oz) Cheddar
   cheese, grated
½ small onion, skinned
   and grated

50 g (2 oz) butter or
   margarine, softened
2.5 ml (½ level tsp)
   mustard powder
salt and pepper
1 tomato, sliced

Wash and trim the cutlets. Put the cheese, onion, butter, mustard and seasoning in a bowl, and mix well together ■ Place the cod steaks on the grill rack and grill under a medium heat for about 5 minutes, turn them and grill for about a further 3 minutes or until almost cooked through ■ Spread the cheese mixture over the fish and grill for 2–3 minutes until golden brown and bubbling. Place a slice of tomato on each cutlet, heat quickly and serve at once.

MEAT

The price of meat varies according to the type of cut, the lean tender parts usually being the most expensive. These cuts can be roasted, fried or grilled, while the tougher parts need slower cooking methods to soften them. The cheaper cuts are just as nutritious as the dearer ones and have an equally good flavour if cooked appropriately.

BEEF

HOW TO CHOOSE BEEF

Lean beef should be bright red, the fat creamy to yellow ■ There should be small flecks of fat through the lean; this fat (called 'marbling') helps to keep the lean moist and tender when the meat is cooking ■ Avoid meat with a line of gristle between lean and fat, which usually suggests it has come from an old animal.

CUTS AND METHODS OF COOKING

Sirloin   A large joint from the loin end of the ribs, usually sold on the bone, but it can also be boned and rolled. It is roasted or cut into steaks (see below).
With bone, allow 225–350 g (8–12 oz) per person.
Without bone, allow 175–225 g (6–8 oz) per person.

Rib   A fairly large joint, next to the sirloin; it can be bought on the bone or boned and rolled, and is roasted. Can also be used for pot roasting, braising and boiling. Quantities as for sirloin.

Topside   A very lean boneless joint, which is usually sold with a layer of fat tied around it. It can be roasted, braised or pot roasted.
Allow 175–225 g (6–8 oz) per person.

Silverside   A boneless joint needing long, slow cooking, such as boiling or braising. Often salted and cooked as traditional boiled beef and carrots.
Allow 175–225 g (6–8 oz) per person.

Brisket   Can be sold on or off the bone and is often salted. It is rather a fatty joint from the breast, but has a good flavour. Brisket can be slow-roasted or braised; when salted, it should be boiled.
With bone, allow 225–350 g (8–12 oz) per person.
Without bone, allow 175–225 g (6–8 oz) per person.

Chuck or blade   A cheaper cut, without bone, fairly lean and suitable for stewing, casseroles and pies. Allow 175–225 g (6–8 oz) per person. Often known as braising or stewing steak.

Leg and shin   Cheap, tough cuts, but quite lean and with a good flavour. Long, slow cooking, eg stewing, is needed; these cuts can be used for curries, goulash, stews, meat pies and puddings. Allow 175–225 g (6–8 oz) per person.

Mince   Finely chopped meat, often mixed with vegetables and pulses. Good for hamburgers, pies and bolognese sauce. Allow 175–225 g (6–8 oz) per person.

ACCOMPANIMENTS

With roast beef serve Yorkshire pudding (see page 103) and horseradish sauce or mustard.

STEAK

PREPARATION OF STEAKS FOR COOKING

Trim the steak to a good shape if necessary and wipe it well. Sprinkle with salt and pepper before cooking. If there is doubt as to its tenderness the steak can be beaten with a rolling pin or steak hammer.

Rump steak   The joint next to the sirloin and one of the commonest cuts used for grilling or frying.

Fillet steak   The undercut of the sirloin, probably one of the best known and most expensive of the cuts used for frying and grilling. Very tender, although it usually has less flavour than rump.

Sirloin steak   Cut into two parts. Porterhouse steak is cut from the thick end of the sirloin, giving a large juicy piece that can weigh 850 g (30 oz); when it is cooked on the bone it is called T-bone steak.

Minute steak is a very thin steak from the upper part of the sirloin, weighing about 150–175 g (5–6 oz), without any fat.

Entrecôte   A steak cut from between the ribs of beef, but a slice cut from the sirloin or rump is often served under this name.

BEEF

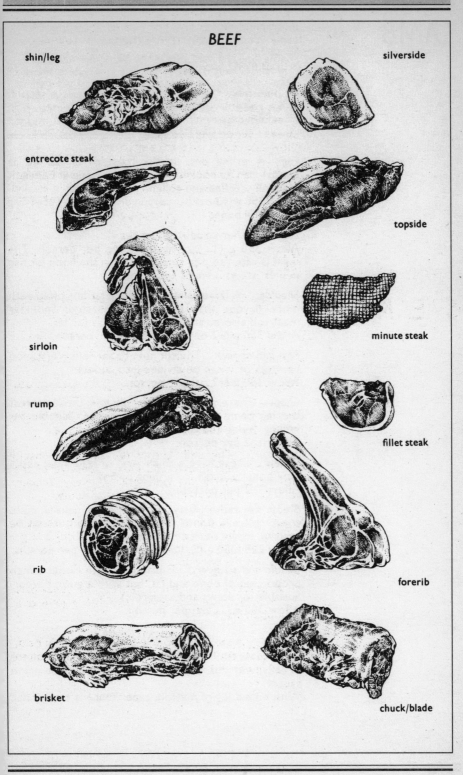

shin/leg

silverside

entrecote steak

topside

sirloin

minute steak

rump

fillet steak

rib

forerib

brisket

chuck/blade

LAMB

HOW TO CHOOSE LAMB

The younger the animal the paler the flesh; in a young lamb it is light pink, while in a mature animal it is light red ■ A slight blue tinge to the bones also suggests the animal is young ■ Imported lamb has a firm, white fat, while English lamb has creamy-coloured fat.

Loin   A prime cut, usually roasted (or served as chops); can be cooked on or off the bone; if boned, it is usually stuffed and rolled.
Allow 350 g (12 oz) per person on the bone; 125–175 g (4–6 oz) if boned.

Leg   Another good roasting cut.
Allow 350 g (12 oz) on the bone per person. The meat is often sold as steaks cut from the bone for use in pies, stews, kebabs and so on.

Shoulder   A large joint, with more fat but often with more flavour than leg. Usually roasted. Shoulder meat can also be sold off the bone, as for leg.
Allow 350 g (12 oz) on the bone per person.

Best end of neck   The cut next to the loin. Very good roasted, or it can be divided into cutlets.
Allow 350 g (12 oz) per person.

Chops   These can be cut from the loin, those nearest the leg being known as chump chops. Suitable for grilling, frying and casseroles.
Allow 1–2 per person.

Cutlets   These have a small 'eye' of lean meat and a long bone; suitable for grilling or frying.
Allow 1–2 per person.

Breast   A rather fatty cut, therefore usually quite cheap. Usually boned, stuffed and rolled; it can be braised, slow-roasted or stewed.
Allow 225–350 g (8–12 oz) on the bone per person.

Middle and scrag end   Cheap cuts with rather a high proportion of bone and fat, but with a good flavour. Suitable for stews and casseroles.
Allow 350 g (12 oz) per person.

ACCOMPANIMENTS

With roast lamb and grilled chops, serve mint sauce or jelly; with roast mutton, redcurrant jelly or onion sauce.
With boiled leg of mutton, caper sauce is traditional.

LAMB

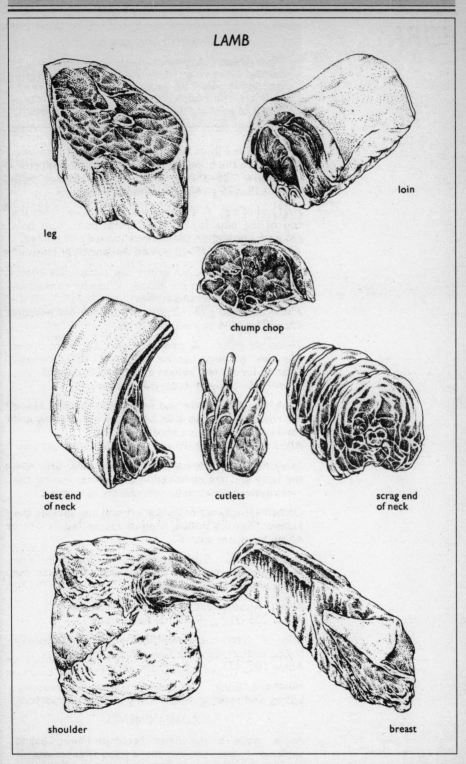

leg

loin

chump chop

best end
of neck

cutlets

scrag end
of neck

shoulder

breast

PORK

Leg   A prime joint but large, so often cut into two. Roasted on the bone, or boned and rolled, with stuffing. Allow 225–350 g (8–12 oz) per person with bone; 125–175 g (4–6 oz) without bone.

Fillet end of leg   A lean, expensive cut taken from the top of the hind leg, with a central bone. It is best roasted, cooked on the bone or boned and stuffed. Allow 225–350 g (8–12 oz) on the bone per person.

Loin   An expensive but prime cut, suitable for roasting; it often includes the kidney. It can be cooked on the bone or boned and stuffed. Allow 225–350 g (8–12 oz) on the bone per person; 125–175 g (4–6 oz) without bone.

Tenderloin (fillet)   A small boneless cut from under the loin, of very tender, lean and delicate meat. Suitable for sautés, kebabs and lightly cooked dishes. Allow 125–175 g (4–6 oz) per person.

Spare rib   Fairly lean and moderately priced. Good for roasting, but can also be cut up for braising and stewing. Also sold as chops or cutlets. Allow 225–350 g (8–12 oz) on the bone per person.

Spare ribs (American and North-country style) are from the belly and are removed in one piece, leaving the meat between the rib bones. Usually barbecued.

Chops   Usually cut from the loin and may include the kidney. They are grilled, fried or casseroled. Allow 1 per person.

Spare rib chops   Cut from the spare rib with little or no bone; usually lean. Cutlets are cooked as for chops. Allow 1 per person.

Blade   Another cut for roasting on the bone. Allow 225–350 g (8–12 oz) per person.

Belly   A fatty cut, sometimes sold salted; usually boiled and served cold. Can also be roasted. Allow 100–175 g (4–6 oz) per person.

Hand and spring   The foreleg, suitable for roasting, boiling and stewing. Allow 350 g (12 oz) per person.

ACCOMPANIMENTS

Apple sauce is the usual accompaniment. Baked apples or redcurrant jelly make good alternatives.

PORK

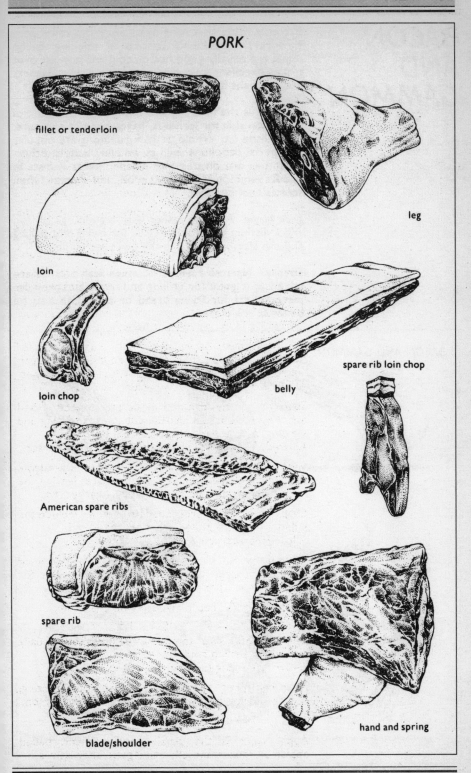

fillet or tenderloin

leg

loin

loin chop

belly

spare rib loin chop

American spare ribs

spare rib

blade/shoulder

hand and spring

BACON AND GAMMON

Bacon is made by curing fresh pork and some goes through the additional process of smoking. Bacon joints are equally good hot or cold and any left over makes excellent savouries or supper dishes. Rashers are excellent for meals from breakfast to supper.

Gammon is the hind leg and the most prized part of the bacon side for leanness, flavour and fine texture. It has little fat. Whole or half gammons are popular for special occasions such as wedding buffets, otherwise they are divided into smaller joints known as middle gammon, corner gammon, and slipper. Often sold as cooked meat.

Back bacon A prime rasher with a good eye of lean and a distinct layer of fat. Used for frying and grilling and can also be bought in the piece for boiling.

Streaky Narrow rashers in which lean and fat are mixed. It is good for grilling and frying and provides plenty of fat for frying bread or eggs. Can also be boiled in the piece.

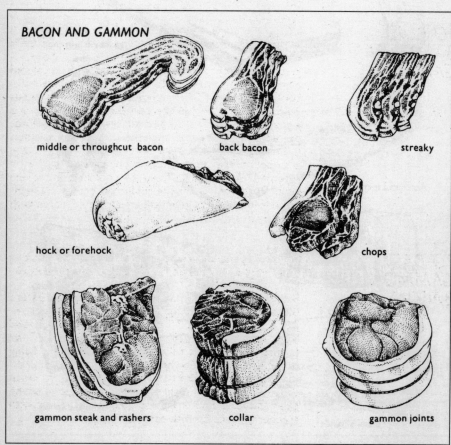

BACON AND GAMMON

middle or throughcut bacon

back bacon

streaky

hock or forehock

chops

gammon steak and rashers

collar

gammon joints

Middle or throughcut Long rashers in which back and streaky are joined. Sold flat or rolled. Good value for family meals and usually priced between back and streaky.

Bacon chops Boneless rib back chops cut between 0.5–1 cm (¼–½ inch) thick. Quick to fry or grill.

Gammon steaks or rashers Gammon steaks about 1 cm (½ inch) thick, almost circular in shape, are the leanest and most expensive cuts for frying and grilling.

Collar Prime collar is one of the best boiling and baking joints and is good for braising. A whole joint weighs about 3.6 kg (8 lb), but it is usually cut into smaller pieces. Collar rashers are substantial and meaty.

Forehock Small boneless forehock pieces are popular for boiling. Can also be bought with the bone in for roasting, boiling, soups and bacon pieces.

TO BOIL BACON OR GAMMON

Weigh the piece, then calculate the cooking time ∎ Tie it if necessary to keep it a good shape. Cover it with water and allow to soak for about 1 hour ∎ Place the joint in a large pan and cover with fresh cold water, bring to the boil, then simmer gently until cooked, allowing 20–25 minutes per 450 g (1 lb) plus 20 minutes ∎ If you are cooking a large joint, eg a gammon of 4.5 kg (10 lb) or over, allow 15–20 minutes per 450 g (1 lb) plus 15 minutes ∎ When the joint is cooked, remove the skin with a knife, if necessary, and serve the meat hot, with parsley sauce ∎ Alternatively, allow the joint to cool in the cooking liquid, cut off the outer skin and press browned breadcrumbs into the fat; when the meat is cold, serve with salad or in sandwiches.

TO BAKE GAMMON OR BACON

After weighing the meat and calculating the cooking time, soak as for boiled bacon. Boil for half the cooking time, then drain the joint and wrap in foil ∎ Bake at 180°C (350°F) mark 4 until 30 minutes before the cooking time is completed. Raise the oven heat to 220°C (425°F) mark 7 ∎ Put 30–45 ml (2–3 level tbsp) brown sugar, 25 g (1 oz) butter and 15 ml (1 tbsp) water in a small saucepan, dissolve and bring to the boil ∎ Undo the foil round the bacon, cut off the skin and score the fat in a diamond pattern. Brush the surface with the sugar glaze; return the joint to the oven and leave until crisp and golden ∎ Serve with cranberry sauce or with canned pineapple.

ROASTING PORK

To prepare the joint, wash it, trim or stuff as necessary, then weigh to calculate the cooking time – see below. Pork rind should be scored, ie cut with a sharp knife, to produce crackling. For a really crisp effect, rub with oil and salt before cooking.

Scoring pork for crackling

ROASTING BEEF, LAMB AND PORK

High temperature roasting at 220°C (425°F) mark 7 is only suitable for really top quality cuts, such as beef fillet. Roasting meat in a moderate oven will produce succulent meat with minimum shrinkage. Bring the meat to room temperature before cooking. Preheat the oven to 180°C (350°F) mark 4. Put the meat in a shallow tin (or on a grid) with the thickest part of any fat uppermost, and roast in the centre of the oven. If there is not much fat, top the meat with 50 g (2 oz) dripping or lard or spoon over oil. Time it as follows:

Beef: 20 minutes per 450 g (1 lb) plus 20 minutes for rare meat; 25 minutes per 450 g (1 lb) plus 25 minutes for medium; 30 minutes per 450 g (1 lb) plus 30 minutes for well done meat.

Lamb: 25 minutes per 450 g (1 lb) plus 25 minutes for medium; 30 minutes per 450 g (1 lb) plus 30 minutes for well done meat.

Pork: All joints should be roasted for 35 minutes per 450 g (1 lb) plus 35 minutes until well done.

BASTING

Several times during the cooking spoon the juices and fat from the meat over the joint – this keeps it moist and gives a good flavour. Put fattier joints – especially pork – on a trivet or grid in the meat tin, to keep the melted fat away from the meat.

COVERED ROASTING

Meat can be cooked in a covered roasting tin. This makes the joint more moist and keeps the oven cleaner, though the flavour and colour are not usually quite so good. Roasting in foil also keeps the meat moist and tender, though again the flavour is not usually so good. Extra cooking time is not needed, but the foil should be opened out for the final 30 minutes, to make the joint brown and crisp.

Basting during cooking

CARVING MEAT

When a joint is well carved it looks attractive and the meat is used in the most economical way. Luckily, carving is an art most people can acquire, given correctly prepared meat and good equipment.

A good butcher will present the joint in the easiest way to carve, if he knows how it is to be served. A joint that includes part of the backbone (eg loin) can be 'chined' – that is, cut through the ribs close to the backbone, leaving a loose piece of bone that is removed before serving.

When preparing meat for cooking never use wooden skewers, which swell and are difficult to remove.

EQUIPMENT

A long-bladed, sharp knife is essential. To restore the sharpness, use a steel or a patent sharpener. To use a steel, draw each side of the blade in turn smoothly down and across with rapid strokes, holding the blade at an angle of 45° to the steel. Take great care, if you are a beginner, not to inflict permanent damage on the knife, and have it expertly reground.

Some stainless steel knives have a hollowed-out, grooved blade; these do not often require sharpening, and are perhaps easier for an inexperienced person, but the skilful carver usually prefers a plain blade.

A sharp two-pronged fork will hold the meat steady; it must have a metal guard to protect the hand in the event of the knife slipping.

A metal meat dish with sharp prongs to hold the joint steady is a great help. Put the meat on the dish with little or no fat and little garnishing. Gravy should be served separately. Place the dish on the table close to the carver and well away from other dishes so that there is room to work.

TECHNIQUE

Each joint must be carved in the way best suited to its structure, to ensure a neat result. The carver must understand the make-up of each joint – where the bone is to be found and how the lean and fat are distributed. The meat is usually best when cut across the grain, though sometimes, when the meat is very tender (as in the undercut of sirloin) the joint is cut with the grain.

It is much easier to carve standing up. Use long, even strokes, keeping the blade at the same angle, to give neat, uniform slices. As you carve, move the knife to and fro, cutting cleanly without bearing down on the meat, which presses out the juices. Serve the meat on to very hot plates or it will cool surprisingly quickly. Beef (except fillet) is carved very thinly, but pork and lamb are cut in slices about 5 mm (¼ inch) thick. When cutting a joint with a bone, always take the knife right up to this, so that eventually the bone is left quite clean.

Sirloin   Stand the joint on its back with the fillet uppermost; remove the strings. Carve the fillet, loosening each slice from the bone with the knife-tip; turn the joint over and carve in long slices right up to the bone.

Carving flank portion   *Cutting towards bone*

Rib of beef   Stand the joint on edge on the bone. Slice downwards along the full length of the joint, cutting each slice down to the bone and slanting a little away from the cut edge so that the bone is left clean. Support the slices with the fork to prevent them breaking.

Cutting fillet   *Cutting wedge-shaped slices*

Boneless joints of beef   Carve across the grain, usually horizontally. In the case of a long piece of roast fillet, however, you will need to carve downwards.

Best end of neck of lamb   Cut the joint right through, downwards, into cutlets. (This joint should be chined.)

Saddle of lamb   First carve the meat from the top of the joint in long slices, cutting downwards and parallel with the backbone. Do this at each end of the bone, then carve diagonal slices from either side of the saddle.

Stuffed breast of lamb   Cut downwards in fairly thick slices, right through the joint.

Leg of lamb Begin by cutting a wedge-shaped slice from the centre of the meatier side of the joint. Carve slices from each side of the cut, gradually turning the knife to get larger slices and ending parallel to the bone. Turn the joint over and carve in long slices.

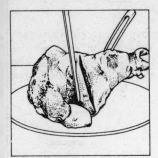

Slicing downwards across joint

Carving down to bone

Removing fat

Shoulder of lamb Cut a thick wedge-shaped slice from the centre of the meatiest side of the joint. Carve small slices from each side down to the shank and the shoulder bone. Turn the joint over and carve in long slices.

Cutting slice from centre

Carving to bone

Carving towards shankbone

Loin of pork Sever the chined bone from the chop bones and put to one side. Divide into chops by cutting between the bones and the scored crackling.

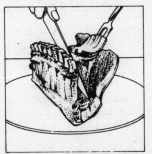

Cutting between chined bone and chops

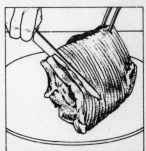

Cutting between bones and crackling

Leg of pork Use the point of the knife to cut through the crackling; it is usually easier to remove it to divide it into portions. Carve as for leg of lamb, but medium thick.

Spare rib of pork Cut between the score marks into moderately thick, even slices.

Boned and rolled pork Remove the string from each part of the joint as it is carved. Cut through the crackling where it was scored half-way along the joint. Lift off the crackling and cut into pieces. Carve the meat into slices.

Lifting off crackling

Carving into slices

HAMBURGERS

Serves 4

450 g (1 lb) lean minced beef, eg chuck, shoulder or rump
½ onion, skinned and grated (optional)

salt and pepper
melted butter or oil for coating or a little fat for shallow frying

Mix the beef well with the onion (if used) and a generous amount of salt and pepper. Shape lightly into 6–8 round, flat cakes ■ To cook, brush sparingly with melted butter or oil and grill each side for 4–6 minutes turning once, or fry in a little fat in a frying pan, turning them once and allowing the same amount of time. Ensure they are cooked right through.

Shaping into flat cakes

GRILLED STEAK

Serves 4

4 steaks
100 g (4 oz) mushrooms
4 tomatoes

butter or margarine
salt and pepper
oil

Trim the steaks. Trim the mushrooms, halve the tomatoes and put a small knob of butter on each half. Season the mushrooms and tomatoes with salt and pepper ■ Brush the steaks with oil, season with salt and pepper and put them under a preheated grill. Cook under a medium heat, turning them regularly, for the times indicated below ■ Lightly grill mushrooms and tomatoes and arrange with steaks on a serving dish.

Cooking times for steaks (in minutes)

Thickness	Rare	Medium Rare	Well-done
2 cm (¾ inch)	5	9–10	12–15
2.5 cm (1 inch)	6–7	10	15
4 cm (1½ inches)	10	12–14	18–20

STEAK AND MUSHROOM PIE

Serves 4

700 g (1½ lb) braising, stewing, chuck or shoulder steak
seasoned flour
1 onion, skinned and chopped
100 g (4 oz) mushrooms, sliced

300 ml (½ pint) beef stock or water
210-g (7½-oz) packet frozen puff pastry, thawed
beaten egg to glaze

Cut the meat in 4-cm (1½-inch) cubes and toss them in the flour. Put the meat, onion and mushrooms in a pan, add just sufficient liquid to cover, put on lid and cook gently over a low heat until tender – about 1½ hours. Cool ■ Transfer the meat and vegetables to a 1.4-litre (2½-pint) pie dish, with enough gravy to half cover ■ Roll out the puff pastry 2.5 cm (1 inch) larger than the top of the dish and cut off a thin strip from the edge of the pie. Damp the rim of the dish, stick on the pastry strip and put on the top, then seal, trim and decorate the edges. Brush the pastry with a little egg. Bake at 220°C (425°F) mark 7 for 20 minutes. Reduce the temperature to 180°C (350°F) mark 4 and cook for a further 20 minutes.

Sticking on pastry strip

Putting on top, sealing

BEEF CASEROLE

Serves 4

Adding liquid to casserole

700 g (1½ lb) stewing
  steak
30 ml (2 tbsp) vegetable
  oil
2 onions, skinned and
  sliced
2–3 carrots, peeled and
  sliced

60 ml (4 level tbsp) plain
  flour
900 ml (1½ pints) beef
  stock
salt and pepper
a bouquet garni

Cut the meat into cubes ■ Heat the oil in a shallow pan and sauté the onions and carrots until golden brown; remove from the pan. Sauté the meat until well browned on all sides. Place the meat and vegetables in a casserole ■ Add the flour to the fat remaining in the pan and cook, stirring, for 1–2 minutes. Add the stock gradually, stirring constantly, then bring to the boil, season and add the bouquet garni. Pour into the casserole and cook in the oven at 170°C (325°F) mark 3 for 2–2½ hours. Remove the bouquet garni before serving.

STEAK AND KIDNEY PUDDING

Serves 4

250 g (9 oz) suetcrust
  pastry (see page 106)
450 g (1 lb) stewing
  steak, cut into 2-cm
  (¾-inch) cubes
2 lamb's kidneys, chopped

15 ml (1 level tbsp) plain
  flour
salt and pepper
1 small onion, skinned
  and chopped
60 ml (4 tbsp) beef stock

Half fill a steamer or large saucepan with water and put it on to boil. Grease a 900-ml (1½-pint) pudding basin ■ Roll the pastry out into a round and cut out a quarter of it to keep for the top. Line the pudding basin with the rest – avoid stretching it ■ Toss the meat and kidney in the seasoned flour. Mix with the onion and put into the basin. Pour in the stock ■ Roll out the remaining pastry into a round the size of the top of the basin and damp the edge. Place on the basin and seal carefully. Cover with greased foil and secure with string, then steam for about 4 hours. Serve with a napkin tied around the basin.

Adding meat

Putting on pastry top

Serving

CURRIED BEEF

Serves 4–6

900g (2 lb) stewing steak
100 g (4 oz) lard or 90 ml (4 tbsp) oil
2 cooking apples, peeled and chopped
4 large onions, skinned and chopped
30 ml (2 level tbsp) curry paste
90 ml (6 level tbsp) plain flour

1 litre (1¾ pints) beef stock or water
salt and pepper
30 ml (2 level tbsp) chutney
100 g (4 oz) sultanas
4 tomatoes, skinned and quartered
a squeeze of lemon juice
boiled rice

Cut the meat into 2-cm (¾-inch) cubes. Heat the fat in a thick-based saucepan and fry the chopped apple and onions until golden ■ Add the meat and fry, stirring all the time, until it is browned. Add the curry paste and flour and fry for 2–3 minutes ■ Gradually add the stock, stir well and boil for 2–3 minutes. Add the seasoning, chutney, sultanas, tomatoes and a squeeze of lemon juice ■ Cover with a close-fitting lid and simmer gently over a low heat for 2–2½ hours, or cook in the oven at 170°C (325°F) mark 3, stirring occasionally to prevent the curry sticking to the base of the pan ■ Before serving, adjust the seasoning as required and place the curry on a hot dish, with a border of boiled rice. Chutney may be served as an accompaniment.

> Raw poultry, various meats and vegetables may also be curried in this way. When making a curry of cooked meat, poultry, eggs or vegetables, or of white fish (which requires less cooking), make the curry sauce, cook it for the full time to blend the flavours, then add the cooked food and heat it in the sauce for about 10–15 minutes. Success in curry-making depends on long, slow cooking.

CHILLI CON CARNE

Serves 4–6

700 g (1½ lb) minced beef
15 ml (1 tbsp) fat or oil
1 large onion, skinned and chopped
1 green pepper, seeded and chopped (optional)
425-g (15-oz) can tomatoes
salt and pepper

15 ml (1 level tbsp) chilli seasoning
15 ml (1 tbsp) vinegar
5 ml (1 level tsp) sugar
30 ml (2 level tbsp) tomato purée
425-g (15-oz) can red kidney beans, drained

Fry the beef in the fat or oil until lightly browned, then add the onion and pepper and fry for 5 minutes until soft ■ Stir in the tomatoes and add the salt and pepper and the chilli seasoning mixed with the vinegar, sugar and tomato purée. Cover and simmer for 2–2½ hours or until tender ■ Add the kidney beans 10 minutes before the end of the cooking time.

COTTAGE PIE

Serves 4

900 g (2 lb) potatoes
45 ml (3 tbsp) milk
knob of butter
salt and pepper
1 large onion, skinned and
    chopped
a little dripping

450 g (1 lb) cold cooked
    beef, minced
150 ml (¼ pint) stock
30 ml (2 tbsp) chopped
    fresh parsley or 10 ml
    (2 level tsp) mixed dried
    herbs

Boil the potatoes, drain and mash them with the milk,
butter and seasoning ■ Fry the onion in a little
dripping for about 5 minutes and mix in the minced
meat, with the stock, seasoning and parsley or mixed
herbs ■ Put the prepared meat mixture into an
ovenproof dish and cover the top with mashed
potato. Mark the top with a fork and bake for 25–30
minutes in the oven at 190°C (375°F) mark 5 until the
surface is crisp and browned.

BOEUF BOUR-GUIGNONNE

Serves 6

50 g (2 oz) butter or
    margarine
30 ml (2 tbsp) vegetable
    oil
125 g (4 oz) streaky
    bacon, rinded and diced
900 g (2 lb) lean braising
    steak, cut into 2.5-cm
    (1-inch) cubes
1 garlic clove, skinned and
    crushed
45 ml (3 level tbsp) flour

salt and pepper
a bouquet garni
150 ml (¼ pint) beef
    stock
300 ml (½ pint) burgundy
    or other red wine
12 small onions, skinned
175 g (6 oz) button
    mushrooms, wiped
chopped parsley, to
    garnish

Melt half the butter and oil in a large flameproof
casserole. Quickly brown the bacon, then drain on
absorbent kitchen paper ■ Reheat the fat and
brown the meat in batches. Return the bacon to the
casserole with the garlic. Sprinkle in the flour and stir
well. Add salt and pepper, the bouquet garni, stock
and wine. Bring to a simmer, stirring, then cover and
cook in the oven at 170°C (325°F) mark 3 for about
2½ hours ■ Meanwhile, fry the onions in the
remaining butter and oil until glazed and golden
brown. Remove from the pan and fry the mushrooms
■ Add the mushrooms and onions to the casserole
and cook for a further 30 minutes. Remove the
bouquet garni, adjust the seasoning. Serve garnished
with chopped parsley.

IRISH STEW

Serves 4

450 g (1 lb) middle neck
  of lamb
900g (2 lb) potatoes,
  peeled and sliced
3 onions, skinned and
  sliced

salt and pepper
beef stock
chopped parsley (optional)

Cut up the meat if necessary and trim off some of the fat. Place alternating layers of meat, potato and onion in a flameproof casserole, finishing with a layer of potato. Season well and add enough stock to half-cover ■ Cover with a lid and simmer very slowly for 3 hours. If you wish, garnish with chopped parsley before serving.

LAMB KEBABS

Serves 4

thick slice of lamb taken
  from the leg – about
  700 g (1½ lb)
45 ml (3 tbsp) olive oil
15 ml (1 tbsp) lemon
  juice
salt and pepper
1 garlic clove, skinned and
  crushed

4 small tomatoes, halved
  (optional)
8 button mushrooms
few bay leaves (optional)
2 small onions, quartered
  (optional)
lemon wedges

Threading skewers

Remove all fat and gristle from the meat and cut it into 2.5-cm (1-inch) cubes. Marinate for 2 hours (or overnight) in the olive oil, lemon juice, seasoning and crushed garlic ■ Thread 8 skewers alternately with meat cubes, halved tomatoes if using, and whole mushrooms. If you like, a bay leaf or an onion quarter may be placed on each side of the meat pieces to give more flavour. Brush with the reserved marinade and cook under a medium grill for 10–15 minutes, turning the kebabs from time to time, until the meat is tender and browned on all sides. Serve on plain boiled rice, with lemon wedges ■ Lamb's kidneys may also be added; allow ½–1 kidney per person, removing the core. Rolled streaky bacon rashers are another good addition to kebabs. For added flavour, include in the marinade some herbs such as dried marjoram and chopped fresh parsley.

A marinade is a seasoned mixture of oil and vinegar, lemon juice or wine, in which food is left for a given time. This helps to soften the fibres of meat or fish, and adds flavour to the food.

NAVARIN OF LAMB

Serves 4

1 kg (2¼ lb) shoulder of lamb
30 ml (2 tbsp) vegetable oil
5 ml (1 level tsp) sugar
15 ml (1 level tbsp) plain flour
900 ml (1½ pints) beef stock or water
30 ml (2 level tbsp) tomato purée
salt and pepper

a bouquet garni
4 onions, skinned and quartered
4 carrots, peeled and sliced
1–2 turnips, peeled and quartered
8 small, even-sized potatoes, peeled
100 g (4 oz) frozen peas (optional)

Trim the meat and cut it into 2.5-cm (1-inch) cubes. Fry it lightly on all sides in the oil. If there is too much fat at this stage, pour off a little to leave 15–30 ml (1–2 tbsp) ■ Stir in the sugar and heat until it browns slightly, then add the flour, stirring until this also cooks and browns. Remove from the heat, stir in the stock gradually, then bring to the boil and add the tomato purée, seasoning and bouquet garni ■ Cover, reduce the heat and simmer for about 1 hour. Remove the bouquet garni, add the onions, carrots and turnips and continue cooking for another 30 minutes. Finally add the potatoes and continue cooking for about 20 minutes, until tender. Add the peas for the last 10 minutes if using ■ Serve the meat on a heated serving dish surrounded by vegetables and garnished with parsley.

MOUSSAKA

Serves 4

2 aubergines, sliced
75–90 ml (5–6 tbsp) olive oil
4–5 medium onions, skinned and sliced
450 g (1 lb) minced raw lamb
4 tomatoes, skinned and sliced

150 ml (¼ pint) beef stock
45 ml (3 level tbsp) tomato purée
2 eggs
45 ml (3 tbsp) milk
45 ml (3 tbsp) cream
salt and pepper

Fry the aubergines in 45–60 ml (3–4 tbsp) of the oil for about 4–5 minutes, then arrange them in the bottom of an ovenproof dish ■ Fry the onions and meat in the remaining oil until lightly browned – about 5 minutes. Place layers of onion and minced meat on top of the aubergines and lastly add the slices of tomato ■ Mix the stock and tomato purée and pour into the dish. Bake in the oven at 180°C (350°F) mark 4 for about 30 minutes ■ Beat together the eggs, milk and cream, season well and pour this mixture over the meat. Put it back into the oven for 15–20 minutes, until the sauce is set and the surface is firm and golden brown.

BARBECUED SPARE RIBS

Serves 4

30 ml (2 tbsp) vegetable oil
175 g (6 oz) onions, skinned and chopped
1 garlic clove, skinned and crushed
30 ml (2 level tbsp) tomato purée
60 ml (4 tbsp) vinegar

1.25 ml (¼ level tsp) dried thyme
1.25 ml (¼ level tsp) chilli seasoning
45 ml (3 level tbsp) honey
1 beef stock cube
1 kg (2¼ lb) spare ribs (American cut)

Heat the oil in a saucepan, add the onion and sauté until softened. Add the flavourings, honey and beef cube, dissolved in 150 ml (¼ pint) hot water. Allow the mixture to simmer gently for 10 minutes ■ Place the spare ribs in a roasting tin in a single layer. Brush with a little of the sauce; roast in the oven at 190°C (375°F) mark 5 for 30 minutes. Pour off the fat and spoon the remaining sauce over the meat; cook for a further 1–1¼ hours.

PORK IN CIDER

Serves 4–6

1.1 kg (2½ lb) boned and rolled lean shoulder or hand of pork, rind and excess fat removed
2 garlic cloves, skinned and cut into slivers
30 ml (2 tbsp) vegetable oil
salt and freshly ground pepper

300 ml (½ pint) dry cider
about 350 g (12 oz) white cabbage
1 large cooking apple
25 g (1 oz) butter
1 onion, skinned and sliced
5 ml (1 tsp) caraway seeds
paprika, to garnish (optional)

With a sharp, pointed knife, make deep incisions in the pork. Insert the garlic slivers, pushing them down into the meat ■ Heat the oil in a large flameproof casserole, add the pork and fry over moderate heat until browned on all sides. Sprinkle with salt and pepper, then pour in the cider and bring very slowly to boiling point ■ Cover the casserole and cook in the oven at 170°C (325°F) mark 3 for 1½ hours ■ Meanwhile, shred the cabbage, cutting away all thick, coarse stalks. Peel and core the apple, then slice it thickly ■ Melt the butter in a saucepan, add the cabbage and apple and fry gently for 5 minutes, tossing the mixture constantly. Stir in the caraway seeds ■ Add the cabbage mixture to the casserole, stirring it into the cooking liquid around the pork. Continue cooking for a further 30 minutes or until the pork is tender. Taste and adjust the seasoning of the cabbage and sauce before serving. Garnish the cabbage with paprika, if liked.

GRILLED PORK CHOPS WITH APPLE RINGS

Serves 4

4 pork chops
olive oil

1 large apple, peeled and
cut in round slices

Trim the chops and brush with oil. Core the apple slices. Place the rings of apple in the base of the grill pan and put the chops on the grid ▪ Grill the chops for 8–10 minutes on each side under a medium grill, to make sure that they are well cooked. When they are done, place on a serving dish and keep hot. Put the apple rings on the grid and brown very lightly. Arrange the apple rings between the chops on a serving dish.

GRILLED KIDNEYS

1–2 lamb's or pig's
  kidneys per person

oil
salt and pepper

Wash the kidneys. Then remove the skin and cut each kidney in half. Cut out the core with sharp scissors ▪ Thread the kidneys on to skewers, cut side uppermost, brush with oil and sprinkle with salt and pepper. Cook under a hot grill for about 6 minutes, uncut side first and then cut side, so that the juices gather in the cut side ▪ Serve on fried bread, with grilled or fried bacon, or with fried potatoes.

Coring kidneys

LIVER, BACON AND MUSHROOMS

Serves 4

450 g (1 lb) lamb's or
  calf's liver
1–2 onions, skinned and
  chopped
4 rashers of lean bacon,
  rinded and chopped

25 g (1 oz) fat or oil
100 g (4 oz) mushrooms,
  sliced

Wash the liver and cut it into thin strips ▪ Fry the onions and bacon in the hot fat or oil for 5 minutes, or until soft, then add the sliced mushrooms and strips of liver and continue frying over a gentle heat, stirring from time to time, for about 5–10 minutes until the meat is just cooked. Drain well before serving.

POULTRY

ROAST TURKEY

Thawing: Frozen turkeys must be thoroughly thawed before cooking. They should be left in their bags and thawed at cool room temperature, not in the fridge. Remove giblets as soon as they are loose – these can be used to make stock for the gravy. To check that the bird is thawed, make sure there are no ice crystals in the body cavity and that the legs are quite flexible. Once it is thoroughly thawed, cover and store in the fridge. Cook as soon as possible.

Stuffing: Loosely stuff the neck end only, not the body cavity of the bird – to ensure that heat penetrates the centre more quickly. Extra stuffing can be baked separately in a covered dish for about 1 hour. Allow about 225 g (8 oz) stuffing for each 2.3 kg (5 lb) dressed weight of turkey and stuff the bird just before cooking. Sew up the neck skin or use skewers; truss bird.

Cooking: Weigh the bird and calculate the cooking time, to be ready 30 minutes before carving. This allows the flesh to firm up, making it easier to slice. Spread with butter or margarine; grind over black pepper. Wrap loosely in foil or put straight into a roasting tin. Preheat the oven to 180°C (350°F) mark 4 and put the turkey in. Fold back the foil about 45 minutes before the end of calculated cooking time to brown. Baste regularly.

Testing: Insert a fine skewer into a turkey thigh. If the juices run clear, it is cooked. If it is not ready, return to the oven to cook a little longer.

*For smaller weights, use turkey roast or drumsticks and cook according to instructions.

Note:
Leftover turkey should be cooled, then refrigerated. Do not leave standing in a warm room.

Oven-ready weight	Approx. thawing time (at room temperature)	Cooking without foil	Cooking foil-wrapped	Approx. no of servings
550 g–1.4 kg* (1¼–3 lb)	4–10 hr	1½–1¾ hr	1¾–2 hr	2–4
1.4–2.3 kg (3–5 lb)	10–15 hr	1¾–2 hr	2–2½ hr	4–8
2.3–3.6 kg (5–8 lb)	15–18 hr	2–2½ hr	2½–3½ hr	8–10
3.6–5 kg (6–11 lb)	18–20 hr	2½–3¼ hr	3½–4 hr	10–15
5–8.8 kg (11–15 lb)	20–24 hr	3¼–3¾ hr	4–5 hr	15–20
8.8–9 kg (15–20 lb)	24–30 hr	3¾–4¼ hr	5–5½ hr	20–30
9–11.3 kg (20–25 lb)	30–36 hr	4¼–4¾ hr	not recommended	30–40
11.3–13.5 kg (25–30 lb)	36–48 hr	4¾–5½ hr	not recommended	40–50

TURKEY STROGANOFF

Serves 4

Igniting brandy with taper

450 g (1 lb) turkey fillet
15 ml (1 tbsp) vegetable
   oil
50 g (2 oz) butter
30 ml (2 tbsp) brandy
   (optional)
1 garlic clove, skinned and
   crushed

salt and pepper
225 g (8 oz) button
   mushrooms, wiped and
   thinly sliced
1 green pepper, seeded
   and thinly sliced
60 ml (4 tbsp) soured
   cream

Thinly slice the turkey ▪ Heat the oil and butter
in a large frying pan and brown the turkey strips.
Add the brandy if using and ignite it with a taper;
when the flames die down, add the crushed garlic and
seasoning ▪ Cover the pan and simmer for 4–5
minutes until the turkey is just tender ▪ Increase
the heat, add the mushrooms and pepper and cook
for 3–4 minutes, turning occasionally ▪ Reduce
the heat, stir in the soured cream (if on the thick
side, stir before adding to the pan) and adjust the
seasoning. Serve hot with rice.

ROAST CHICKEN

Serves 4

1 oven-ready chicken –
   about 1.5 kg (3¼ lb)
forcemeat or sausage
   stuffing (see page 102)

melted butter or oil
salt and pepper
6 rashers of streaky
   bacon, rinded

If the bird is frozen, allow it to thaw completely and
remove the giblets from the inside. Wash the inside
of the bird, dry with absorbent kitchen paper and
stuff it at the neck end. Fold the skin round the neck
opening and catch it under the wing tips; tie the legs
firmly, brush the chicken with melted butter or oil
and sprinkle with salt and pepper. Place 2 rashers of
bacon over the breast ▪ Place in a roasting tin.
Cook in the oven at 200°C (400°F) mark 6, basting
from time to time and allowing 20 minutes per 450 g
(1 lb) plus 20 minutes. Put a piece of greaseproof
paper over the breast if it shows signs of becoming
too brown. Prepare bacon rolls ▪ Using a round
bladed knife stretch the rashers, cut in half and roll
up. Fifteen minutes before the end of cooking,
remove the bacon from the chicken ▪ Place the
bacon rolls in the roasting tin for the remaining
15 minutes. Take the string from the legs before
serving ▪ Put the bird on a dish and garnish with
bacon rolls. Serve bread sauce and gravy separately.

Removing giblets

Stuffing neck end

Tying legs

CORONATION CHICKEN

Serves 8

2.3-kg (5-lb) chicken, cooked
15 ml (1 tbsp) vegetable oil
1 small onion, skinned and finely chopped
15 ml (1 level tbsp) curry paste
15 ml (1 tbsp) tomato purée

100 ml (4 fl oz) red wine
juice of ½ lemon
4 canned apricot halves, finely chopped
300 ml (½ pint) mayonnaise
100 ml (4 fl oz) whipping cream
salt and pepper
watercress to garnish

Remove all the flesh from the chicken and dice. In a small pan, heat the oil and add the onion and cook for about 3 minutes or until softened. Add the curry paste, tomato purée, wine and lemon juice ■ Simmer, uncovered, for about 10 minutes until well reduced. Strain and cool ■ Sieve the chopped apricot to form a purée. Beat the cooked sauce into the mayonnaise with the apricot purée ■ Lightly whip the cream and fold into the mixture. Season, adding a little extra lemon juice if necessary ■ Toss the chicken pieces into the sauce and serve garnished with watercress.

Dicing chicken flesh

Sieving chopped apricot

Folding cream into mixture

CASSEROLE OF CHICKEN

Serves 4

2 medium onions, skinned and sliced
2 sticks celery, trimmed and chopped
100 g (4 oz) mushrooms, sliced
50 g (2 oz) bacon, rinded and chopped
15 ml (1 tbsp) vegetable oil

25 g (1 oz) butter or margarine
4 chicken joints
45 ml (3 level tbsp) plain flour
450 ml (¾ pint) chicken stock
425-g (15-oz) can tomatoes, drained
salt and pepper

Lightly fry the onions, celery, mushrooms and bacon in the oil and butter for about 5 minutes, until golden brown. Remove them from the pan with a slotted spoon and use them to line the bottom of the casserole ■ Fry the chicken joints in the oil and butter for 5 minutes, until golden brown. Put the chicken in the casserole on the bed of vegetables ■ Stir the flour into the fat remaining in the pan and cook for 2–3 minutes; gradually stir in the stock and bring to the boil. Continue to stir until the mixture thickens then add the tomatoes, with salt and pepper to taste ■ Pour this sauce over the chicken joints, cover and cook in the oven at 180°C (350°F) mark 4 for ¾–1 hour, until the chicken is tender.

CREAMY CHICKEN AND TARRAGON PIE

Serves 4

25 g (1 oz) butter or margarine
25 g (1 oz) flour
300 ml (½ pint) milk
salt and pepper
450 g (1 lb) cold cooked chicken, cut into cubes
2.5 ml (½ level tsp) dried tarragon

198-g (7-oz) can sweetcorn, drained
150 ml (¼ pint) soured cream
212-g (7½-oz) packet puff pastry, thawed
beaten egg to glaze

Melt the butter in a pan and stir in the flour. Cook for 2 minutes, stirring. Remove from the heat and stir in the milk. Bring the sauce to the boil and cook for 2 minutes, stirring continuously. Season well and stir in the chicken, tarragon, sweetcorn and soured cream. Pour into a 1.1-litre (2-pint) pie dish ■ Roll out the pastry 5 cm (2 inches) wider than the dish. Cut a 2.5-cm (1-inch) strip from the outer edge and use to line the dampened rim of the pie dish. Dampen the pastry rim with water and cover with the pastry lid, sealing the edges well. Trim and finish. Brush with beaten egg to glaze ■ Bake in the oven at 200°C (400°F) mark 6 for about 30 minutes until the pie crust is golden brown and well risen. Serve hot or cold with a salad of green vegetables.

VEGETABLES AND SALADS

> ### PREPARATION OF POTATOES
> Wash old potatoes well, then peel thinly with a knife or potato peeler and cut into even-sized pieces. Wash and scrape the skins off new potatoes, or just brush thoroughly. As soon as they have been prepared, put them into cold water until wanted for cooking, to prevent them discolouring.

Boiled potatoes

175–225 g (6–8 oz) potatoes per person
salt

butter or margarine
chopped parsley

Put the potatoes into salted water and simmer until cooked but unbroken – 10–15 minutes for new potatoes, 15–20 minutes for old ones ■ Drain well, toss with a knob of butter or margarine and serve sprinkled with parsley.

Mashed potatoes

175–225 g (6–8 oz) old potatoes per person

salt

Boil the potatoes as above. Drain well, then mash with a potato masher or fork until smooth and quite free from lumps.

Mashing potatoes

Creamed potatoes

175–225 g (6–8 oz) old
   potatoes per person
salt
butter or margarine

45–60 ml (3–4 tbsp) milk
salt and pepper
chopped parsley

Boil the potatoes as before, then mash until smooth, adding a knob of butter or margarine, the milk and a little extra seasoning if necessary. Return them to a gentle heat and beat well with a wooden spoon until fluffy ■ Serve sprinkled with chopped parsley.

Potatoes baked in their jackets

1 even-sized potato per
   person – about 275 g
   (10 oz)

butter or soured cream to
   serve

Scrub each potato well and prick all over with a fork. Bake in the oven at 200°C (400°F) mark 6, for about 1–1¼ hours, or until they feel soft when squeezed ■ Cut a cross in the top of each potato, put in a knob of butter or a spoonful of soured cream, and serve at once.

Chipped potatoes

Cutting potatoes into strips

175–225 g (6–8 oz) old
   potatoes per person

oil for deep frying

Wash and peel the potatoes, then cut into 0.5–1-cm (¼–½-inch) slices. Cut these slices into long strips of 0.5–1 cm (¼–½ inch) wide. (Several slices can be put on top of one another and cut together for speed.) ■ Place in cold water and leave for at least 30 minutes; drain well and dry with a cloth ■ Heat the oil in a deep saucepan or fryer to 190°C (375°F), or until a chip dropped into the fat rises to the surface straight away, surrounded by bubbles ■ Put enough chips into the basket to about quarter-fill it and lower into the oil ■ Cook for 6–7 minutes. Remove the chips and drain on kitchen paper. Repeat until all the chips are cooked ■ Just before serving, reheat the oil and fry the chips rapidly for about 3 minutes until crisp and golden outside and tender inside. Drain well on kitchen paper and serve in an uncovered dish.

Roast potatoes

175–225 g (6–8 oz) old
   potatoes per person

lard, dripping or oil

Wash and peel the potatoes, then cut into even-sized pieces. Cook in salted water for 2–3 minutes (depending on size). Drain well, then carefully transfer to a roasting tin containing a thin layer of hot lard or dripping. Baste well and bake in the oven at 220°C

(425°F) mark 7 for 45 minutes to 1 hour, basting occasionally and turning once or twice, until tender inside and crisp and brown outside. Drain well on kitchen paper, put into a serving dish, sprinkle with salt and serve at once.

If preferred, the potatoes need not be parboiled first (in this case they will take longer to cook); they may also be cooked in the roasting tin around the meat, when little or no extra fat will be needed.

Scalloped potatoes

Serves 4

700 g (1½ lb) potatoes, peeled and finely sliced
salt and pepper
45 ml (3 level tbsp) flour

25 g (1 oz) butter or margarine
150 ml (¼ pint) milk

Arrange the potatoes in layers in a greased oven-proof dish. Season each layer, dredge with flour and dot with butter ■ Repeat the layers until all the slices are used, then pour over the milk. Cook in the oven at 190°C (375°F) mark 5 for about 1¼ hours, until the potatoes are cooked and the top golden brown.

Spring greens

Separate the leaves and cut off the base of any thick stems. Wash well, then shred roughly. Cook as for cabbage. Chop before serving if you wish.
Allow 225 g (8 oz) per person.

Brussels sprouts

Remove the outer leaves, cut a cross in the bottom of the stems, wash, then cook rapidly in boiling salted water for about 10–15 minutes, or until just cooked. Drain well, then toss with a little butter or margarine and a sprinkling of pepper.
Allow 100–175 g (4–6 oz) per person.

Cutting cross in stems

Marrow

Peeling marrow

Peel the marrow, remove the seeds and cut the flesh into large cubes. Cook in a little boiling salted water for 10–15 minutes, until soft; drain really well. Toss with butter and a sprinkling of pepper and chopped parsley or coat with a well-seasoned white or cheese sauce (see page 98).

Alternatively, cut the marrow into large dice; melt about 25 g (1 oz) butter in a saucepan, add the marrow, season and cover tightly. Cook over a low heat, shaking the pan occasionally, for about 10 minutes. Garnish with chopped parsley.

Marrow can also be roasted in the dripping round the meat or stuffed and baked either whole or in rings (see page 71).

Allow 175 g (6 oz) per portion.

Savoy and Dutch cabbage

Remove the coarse outer leaves, cut the cabbage in half and cut out the hard centre stalk. Wash thoroughly, shred the leaves finely, and cook rapidly in about 2.5 cm (1 inch) boiling salted water for 5–10 minutes, or until just done. Drain well and toss with a knob of butter or margarine, a sprinkling of pepper and a pinch of grated nutmeg (optional). Serve at once.

Allow 175–225 g (6–8 oz) per person.

For salads, wash the leaves in cold salted water. Drain well and shred finely.

Cutting out centre stalk

Shredding leaves

Red cabbage   Cook as above but add 15 ml (1 tbsp) vinegar to the water to improve the flavour; allow 15–20 minutes cooking.

Spinach

Remove the stalks and any damaged leaves and wash very thoroughly in several changes of water, to remove grit or mud. Pack it into a saucepan with only the water that clings to it, heat gently turning the spinach occasionally, then bring to the boil and cook gently for 5–10 minutes until tender. Drain thoroughly, add a small knob of butter or margarine and some salt and pepper before serving.

Allow at least 225 g (8 oz) per person.

Cauliflower

Remove any coarse outer leaves, but leave the small ones intact. Trim the base of the stem and cut a cross in it, then wash the cauliflower well. Cook, stem side down, in fast-boiling salted water to come half way up for 10–15 minutes, depending on the size. Drain well and, if liked, serve coated with a white or cheese sauce (see page 98).

The cauliflower can be divided into individual florets and cooked in fast-boiling water for 8–10 minutes. Drain well and serve tossed with butter or margarine and a sprinkling of pepper or coated with sauce.

A medium cauliflower serves 4 people.

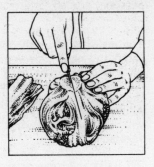

Cutting cross in base of stem

Courgettes

These are normally cooked unpeeled, either left whole or cut into rounds. They may be cooked in a minimum of boiling water for about 5 minutes, steamed or fried. They are served with melted butter and chopped parsley or tarragon. Alternatively, cook, dress with French dressing while still warm, then leave to go cold and serve as a salad.

Allow 100 g (4 oz) per portion.

French and runner beans

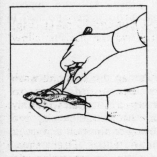

French Top, tail and wash the beans. Cook whole, or cut in half if large, in boiling salted water until tender but still crisp – 8–12 minutes for young beans, 15 minutes for larger ones.

Runner Top, tail and string the beans. Cut diagonally into 1-cm (½-inch) slices or slice thinly lengthways. Cook in boiling salted water for about 10 minutes until tender.

French and runner beans should be served tossed in butter or margarine with a sprinkling of pepper.

Allow 100–225 g (4–8 oz) per person.

Stringing the beans

Peas

Shell the peas, wash and place in boiling salted water with a little sugar and a sprig of fresh mint. Cook till tender – 8–10 minutes; drain, take out the mint and add a small knob of butter or margarine.
Allow about 225 g (8 oz) peas in the pod per person.

Broad beans

Shell the beans, cook them in boiling salted water for about 10 minutes until tender and drain. Serve with parsley sauce or tossed with a knob of butter or margarine and a little chopped parsley.
Allow 225–350 g (8–12 oz) beans in the shell per person.

Mushrooms

The majority of mushrooms bought today are cultivated and need only wiping before being used. Cut off and discard the earthy end of each stalk. Field mushrooms need skinning and should be washed thoroughly to remove any mud or grit.
Allow 25–75 g (1–3 oz) per person, depending on whether the mushrooms are used as a garnish or a vegetable.
For salads, wipe or skin as necessary, trim the base of the stalks and halve or slice.

Wiping the mushrooms

Grilled Wipe the mushrooms and trim the stalks level with the caps. Melt 50 g (2 oz) butter or margarine per 450 g (1 lb) mushrooms. Dip the caps in butter and grill cap uppermost for 2 minutes. Turn them, sprinkle with salt and pepper and grill for a further 2–3 minutes.

Sauté Prepare the mushrooms, leaving them whole or cutting in slices as preferred. Cook gently until soft in about 25 g (1 oz) butter or margarine with some salt and pepper; shake them from time to time. A squeeze of lemon juice can be added just before serving.

Slicing mushrooms

Baked Place the prepared whole mushrooms stalks uppermost, in a greased ovenproof dish, dot with butter or margarine, add a little salt and pepper, then cover with foil or greaseproof paper and bake in the oven at 190°C (375°F) mark 5 for 15–20 minutes, or until cooked.

Turnips

Peel rather thickly, cut either in pieces or dice and put immediately under water to prevent discoloration. Cook in salted water until tender; the time will vary considerably, from 20–30 minutes, according to their age and whether the pieces are large or small. Drain and add pepper and a little butter or margarine; they may also be mashed. Young turnips may be left whole.
Allow 175–225 g (6–8 oz) per person.

Parsnips

Peel these thinly and cut into quarters, or into even-sized pieces if large and remove any hard centre core. They are very good cooked in the dripping round roast meat – first blanch in boiling water for 2 minutes, then drain and roast for about 30 minutes. Otherwise, boil them in salted water until tender, allowing about 15–20 minutes. Drain and toss with a knob of butter or margarine and some grated nutmeg or chopped parsley. Alternatively, mash the parsnips well with butter and pepper.
Allow 175–225 g (6–8 oz) per person.

Carrots

Dice, strips, rounds

New Trim off the leaves, then scrape lightly with a sharp knife. Small new carrots are usually cooked whole. Simmer in salted water for about 15 minutes or until cooked and serve tossed with a little butter or margarine, pepper and chopped parsley.

Old Peel thinly and cut into 0.5–1-cm (¼–½-inch) lengthways strips; these strips can then be cut across into small dice. Alternatively, cut them into thin rounds. Simmer in salted water until tender – about 10 minutes for strips and cubes, 6–8 minutes for thin slices.
For salads, pare and cut into thin rings if new, or grate (using the large holes of the grater) if old.
Allow 175–225 g (6–8 oz) per person.

Leeks

Remove the coarse outer leaves and cut off the roots and green tops. Split the leaf end down so that the leeks can be thoroughly washed and any soil or grit removed. Cook in boiling salted water until just tender – about 8–10 minutes – then drain very thoroughly.
Allow 1–3 leeks or 225–350 g (8–12 oz) per person, depending on the amount of waste.

Trimming roots and splitting leaves

Swedes

These are prepared and cooked like turnips. They are sometimes diced and cooked with diced turnips or carrots.
Allow 175–225 g (6–8 oz) per person.

Beetroot

Cut off the leaves, leaving 2.5 cm (1 inch) of stem and taking care not to damage the skins. Wash the beetroot and boil them in salted water until tender; small, early beetroot will take about 30 minutes, larger, older ones about 1½ hours. Peel off the skin, cut off the stems and roots and cut the beetroot into cubes or slices; serve hot, coated with a white sauce, or leave to cool, then serve sliced in a little vinegar.

Beetroot can be bought ready cooked. Peel thinly, then dice or grate. Put in a small dish, sprinkle with salt and pepper and cover with vinegar.

Allow 100 g (4 oz) per person.

Celery

Washing celery with brush

Wash celery thoroughly, using a brush to remove all soil from the grooves of the outer stalks. Cut the stalks in even lengths and cook in boiling salted water until tender, 10–20 minutes depending on the coarseness of the celery. Drain carefully and serve with a white, parsley or cheese sauce (see page 98).

Allow 1 head of celery per person if small, 2–3 sticks if large.

For salad, separate the sticks and scrub well in cold water to remove any dirt. Slice, chop or make into 'curls', as follows. Cut into strips about 0.5 cm (¼ inch) wide and 5 cm (2 inches) long. Make cuts along the length of each strip, close together and to within 1 cm (½ inch) of one end. Leave the pieces in cold water for 1–2 hours, until the strips curl.

Tomatoes

Grilled Choose even-sized tomatoes; halve and place on the grid in the grill pan, cut side uppermost. Put a small piece of butter or margarine and a sprinkling of salt and pepper on each and cook under medium heat for 5–10 minutes, depending on their size, until soft.

Baked Prepare as for grilled tomatoes or if of even size leave whole and cut a cross just through the skin, on the end away from the stem. Place in a greased ovenproof dish. Brush with melted butter or margarine and sprinkle with salt and pepper, cover with foil or greaseproof paper and bake in the oven at 180°C (350°F) mark 4 for 10–15 minutes.

Allow 1–2 tomatoes per person, or 450 g (1 lb) for 4.

Peeling off tomato skin

TO SKIN TOMATOES

Dip them in a pan of boiling water for 20–30 seconds, then place in a basin of cold water – the skin should then peel off easily.

For salads, slice thinly or cut into wedges.

Onions

Trim the roots and remove the thin, papery brown skin. Cook in boiling salted water for 20–30 minutes according to size, drain well and serve with a white or cheese sauce (see page 98).
Allow 100–175 g (4–6 oz) per person.
For salads use spring onions. Trim off the root end, remove the papery outer skins and trim the green leaves down to about 5 cm (2 inches).

Removing outer skin of onion

Lettuce

Separate the leaves and wash them under a running cold tap or in a bowl of clean water. Drain the lettuce by shaking it in a clean tea-towel or colander.

Cucumber

Wipe the skin and either leave it on or peel very thinly. Cut into very thin slices. To give a deckled effect, cut thin strips from the skin with a sharp knife before slicing the cucumber.

Cress

Trim off the roots and lower part of the stems with scissors and place the leaves in a colander or sieve. Wash (under a fast-running cold tap, if possible), turning the cress over to remove any seeds. Drain.

Watercress

Trim the coarse ends from the stalks and place the watercress in a bowl of cold water, adding 10 ml (2 level tsp) salt. Drain well.

Trimming ends from stalks

Herbs (eg parsley or mint)

Remove any large stems, wash the leaves in a colander or sieve, shake and allow to drain well, then chop with a cook's knife.

Radishes

Trim off the root end and leaves, place the radishes in cold water and rub well to remove any dirt. Leave whole, if small; if large, slice thinly into rings or make into flowers.

Trimming and slicing

FRENCH DRESSING

salt and pepper
2.5 ml (½ level tsp) mustard
a pinch of sugar

15 ml (1 tbsp) vinegar
45 ml (3 tbsp) olive or vegetable oil

Put the salt, pepper, mustard and sugar together in a basin, add the vinegar and mix well, then blend in the olive oil, using a fork.
This is the dressing most commonly used for green salads (see page 69) and for simple mixed salads. It may be varied in several ways – for example:

With parsley or other herbs or flavourings   Make French dressing in the usual way and add some freshly chopped parsley, chervil or other fresh herbs. Chopped capers or crushed garlic can also be included in the dressing, to add interest and flavour.

With chopped olives   Chop a few stuffed olives and add to French dressing made as above.

MAYONNAISE

Makes about
150 ml (¼ pint)

1 egg yolk
2.5 ml (½ level tsp) dry mustard
salt and pepper
2.5 ml (½ level tsp) sugar

about 150 ml (¼ pint) olive or vegetable oil
15 ml (1 tbsp) white wine vinegar or lemon juice

Put the egg yolk in a basin with the seasonings and sugar. Mix thoroughly, then add the oil drop by drop, stirring briskly with a wooden spoon the whole time or using a whisk, until the sauce is thick and

Adding oil drop by drop

smooth ■ If it becomes too thick add a little of the vinegar. When all the oil has been added, add the vinegar or lemon juice gradually and mix thoroughly.

> To keep the basin firmly in position while you whisk in the oil, twist a damp cloth tightly round the base. Should the sauce curdle while you are making it, put another egg yolk into a basin and add the curdled sauce very gradually, in the same way as the oil is added to the original egg yolk.

GREEN SALAD

Use two or more salad leaves, such as lettuce, cress, watercress, rocket, lamb's lettuce, endive, chicory or cabbage. Wash and drain them and just before serving toss lightly in a bowl with French dressing (see page 68), adding a little finely chopped onion if you wish ■ Sprinkle with chopped fresh parsley, chives, mint, tarragon or other herbs as available.

COLESLAW

Serves 4

¼ of a hard white
   cabbage
½ a green pepper
2–3 sticks of celery

1 red-skinned eating
   apple
mayonnaise (see page 68)

Shred the cabbage finely, cut the pepper into thin strips, chop the celery and dice the apple or cut in segments ■ Mix all these ingredients together and bind with mayonnaise. Serve garnished with a few strips of green pepper and segments of apple.
Note: 25–50 g (1–2 oz) finely chopped walnuts or 50 g (2 oz) sultanas can be included.

ORANGE SALAD

Serves 4

2 oranges
a little chopped tarragon
   and chervil, or chopped
   mint
10 ml (2 tsp) wine vinegar

15 ml (1 tbsp) olive or
   vegetable oil
5 ml (1 tsp) lemon juice
watercress to garnish

Peel the oranges, removing all the skin and white pith, and cut into segments or cut them across thinly into rounds using a serrated knife ■ Put them into a shallow dish and sprinkle with a mixture of chopped tarragon and chervil, or with mint ■ Blend together the oil, vinegar and lemon juice, pour over the fruit and allow to stand for a short time ■ To serve, lay the oranges on a bed of watercress and spoon the dressing over.

TOMATO AND BASIL SALAD

Serves 4

450 g (1 lb) ripe
   tomatoes
15–30 ml (1–2 tbsp)
   chopped fresh basil
a little chopped onion
   (optional)

salt and pepper
45 ml (3 tbsp) olive or
   vegetable oil
15 ml (1 tbsp) balsamic
   or wine vinegar

Slice the tomatoes fairly thinly ■ Arrange in a dish
and sprinkle with the chopped basil, and onion, if
using ■ Season with salt and pepper and drizzle
the oil and vinegar over the tomatoes ■ Cover
and leave in the refrigerator for 1 hour before
serving.

MUSTARDY POTATO SALAD

Serves 4

700 g (1½ lb) small new
   potatoes, scrubbed
salt and pepper

Dressing:
225 ml (8 fl oz) fromage
   frais

75 ml (5 tbsp)
   mayonnaise
30 ml (2 tbsp) wholegrain
   mustard
10 ml (2 tsp) Dijon
   mustard
chopped fresh parsley or
   chives

Cook the potatoes in their skins in boiling salted
water for about 10 minutes or until tender ■
Meanwhile, mix together the ingredients for the
dressing and season to taste with salt and pepper ■
Drain the potatoes and immediately toss with the
dressing. Allow to cool before serving.

GREEK SALAD

Serves 4–6

700 g (1½ lb) tomatoes
1 cucumber, halved and
   sliced
1 large green pepper,
   seeded and cut into
   strips
225 g (8 oz) feta cheese,
   diced
125 g (4 oz) black olives,
   pitted

Dressing:
135 ml (9 tbsp) olive oil
45 ml (3 tbsp) lemon
   juice
15 ml (1 tbsp) chopped
   oregano
large pinch of sugar
pepper

Slice the tomatoes and place in a serving bowl with
the cucumber, green pepper, feta and olives ■
Whisk the dressing ingredients together in a jug or
shake together in a screw-topped jar ■ Pour the
dressing over the salad and toss gently. Serve at
once.

SUPPER DISHES

MUSHROOMS ON TOAST

Serves 2

225 g (8 oz) mushrooms
15 ml (1 tbsp) lemon
  juice or 5 ml (1 tsp)
  Worcestershire sauce
25 g (1 oz) butter

salt and pepper
a little cream or top of the
  milk
fingers of hot toast
chopped fresh parsley

Chop the mushrooms, put them in a small pan and add the lemon juice or Worcestershire sauce and butter; season to taste. Cook gently until the liquid has evaporated, then keep hot ■ Just before serving, stir in the cream or top of the milk, place the mixture on the fingers of toast and garnish with a little chopped parsley.

CHICKEN LIVERS ON TOAST

Serves 2

75–100 g (3–4 oz)
  chicken livers
seasoned flour
butter for frying

50 g (2 oz) sliced
  mushrooms (optional)
½ glass sherry or Madeira
2 slices bread, toasted

Wash and dry the livers, cut them in small pieces and coat with the seasoned flour ■ Melt some butter in a frying pan and fry the bread for 2–3 minutes, until golden on both sides. Put in the prepared livers and mushrooms if used and stir them over the heat until browned ■ Add the sherry or Madeira, mix and cook for 10–15 minutes. Serve on toast.

STUFFED MARROW

Serves 4

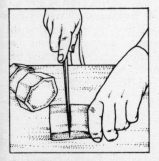

Cutting into slices

1 marrow, about 1 kg
  (2¼ lb)
350 g (12 oz) cold
  cooked meat, minced
60 ml (4 level tbsp) fresh
  breadcrumbs
1 onion, skinned and
  finely chopped

5–10 ml (1–2 level tsp)
  mixed dried herbs or 15
  ml (1 tbsp) chopped
  fresh parsley
salt and pepper
1 egg, beaten
tomato sauce (see page
  101)

Wash the marrow, peel and cut into slices 4–5 cm (1½–2 inches) thick. Remove the seeds and stand the pieces in a greased ovenproof dish ■ Mix the minced meat, crumbs, onion, herbs and seasoning with a fork and add enough egg to bind together ■ Put the stuffing into the marrow rings, cover with foil and bake in the oven at 180°C (350°F) mark 4 for 20 minutes or until tender. Serve with tomato sauce.

STUFFED AUBERGINES

Serves 4

2 medium aubergines
50 g (2 oz) cooked ham, chopped
15 ml (1 tbsp) chopped fresh parsley
1 tomato, skinned and chopped
50 g (2 oz) fresh breadcrumbs
½ onion, skinned and grated
salt and pepper
100 g (4 oz) Cheddar cheese, grated
a little stock or beaten egg

Wash the aubergines and remove the stalks. Cut in half lengthways and scoop out the flesh from the centre of each, leaving a 0.5-cm (¼-inch) thick 'shell' ■ Make the stuffing by combining the ham, parsley, tomato, crumbs, onion, seasoning and half the grated cheese with the roughly chopped aubergine flesh. Moisten with a little stock or beaten egg and fill the aubergine shells ■ Sprinkle with the remaining grated cheese, cover with a lid or foil and bake in the oven at 200°C (400°F) mark 6 for 30 minutes, or until cooked. Uncover and cook for a further 5–10 minutes, until crisp and brown on top. Serve hot with a cheese or tomato sauce (see pages 98 and 101).

QUICHE LORRAINE

Serves 4

shortcrust pastry made with 150 g (5 oz) flour (see page 104)
75–100 g (3–4 oz) lean bacon, rinded and chopped
75–100 g (3–4 oz) Gruyère or Cheddar cheese, thinly sliced
2 eggs, beaten
150 ml (¼ pint) single cream or milk
salt and pepper

Roll out the pastry and use it to line an 18-cm (7-inch) plain flan ring or sandwich cake tin ■ Cover the bacon with boiling water and leave for 2–3 minutes, then drain well. Put into the pastry case with the cheese; mix the eggs and cream, season well and pour into the case ■ Bake in the oven at 200°C (400 °F) mark 6 for about 30 minutes, until well risen and golden.

VEGETARIAN DISHES

QUICK PIZZA

Serves 2–3

100 g (4 oz) self-raising
flour
2.5 ml (½ level tsp) salt
75 ml (5 tbsp) vegetable
oil
45–60 ml (3–4 tbsp)
water
I small onion, skinned
and chopped
5–10 ml (1–2 level tsp)
dried mixed herbs

396-g (14-oz) can
tomatoes, drained and
chopped or 450g (1 lb)
fresh tomatoes, skinned
and chopped
25 g (1 oz) butter or
margarine
100 g (4 oz) Cheddar
cheese, cut in small
cubes
few olives and/or canned
artichoke hearts

Spreading cheese

Mix the flour and salt and stir in 15 ml (1 tbsp) oil and
enough water to mix to a fairly soft dough. Roll out
to an 18-cm (7-inch) round and fry on one side in the
remaining oil in a large frying pan ■ Meanwhile
make the topping by frying the onion, herbs and
tomatoes in the butter or margarine. Turn the dough
over and spread with the tomato mixture, the cheese
and a few sliced olives and/or artichoke hearts ■
Fry until the underside is golden and place under a
hot grill until the cheese is golden and bubbling. Serve
hot, cut in wedges.

BOSTON BAKED BEANS

Serves 6–8

450 g (1 lb) dried haricot
beans, soaked overnight
2 onions, skinned and
chopped
30 ml (2 tbsp) Dijon
mustard
30 ml (2 tbsp) dark
brown sugar
75 ml (5 tbsp) black
treacle
450 ml (¾ pint) tomato
juice

450 ml (¾ pint) lager
60 ml (4 tbsp) tomato
purée
60 ml (4 tbsp) vegetarian
Worcestershire sauce
30 ml (2 tbsp) chilli sauce
I garlic clove, skinned and
crushed
salt and pepper

Drain the beans. Put them in a large flameproof casserole
and add enough fresh cold water to cover. Bring to the
boil and boil rapidly for 10 minutes, then simmer for 45
minutes ■ Drain and return to the casserole, adding
the remaining ingredients. Mix well, season with salt and
pepper, cover with a tight-fitting lid and cook in the oven
at 150°C (300°F) mark 2 for 4 hours or until the beans are
very tender ■ Check and stir the beans occasionally
during cooking and add a little water, if necessary, to prevent them drying out. Check the seasoning before serving.

COURGETTE AND CHEESE FLAN

Serves 4–6

175 g (6 oz) plain flour
15 ml (1 level tbsp) grated Parmesan cheese
2.5 ml (½ level tsp) dry mustard
1.25 ml (¼ level tsp) paprika
175 g (6 oz) butter or margarine
about 30 ml (2 tbsp) cold water
450 g (1 lb) small courgettes, trimmed and sliced

1 garlic clove, skinned and crushed
grated rind of ½ a lemon
10 ml (2 tsp) lemon juice
salt and pepper
45 ml (3 level tbsp) plain flour
150 ml (¼ pint) milk
142 ml (5 fl oz) soured cream
1 egg, separated
175 g (6 oz) mature Cheddar cheese, grated
snipped chives to garnish

Sift the flour, Parmesan, mustard and paprika together. Rub in half the fat with your fingertips, add about 30 ml (2 tbsp) cold water and draw the dough together with your fingertips ■ Roll it out and use to line a 23-cm (9-inch) fluted flameproof flan dish. Bake blind (see page 106) in the oven at 200°C (400°F) mark 6 for about 20 minutes ■ Blanch the courgettes for 1 minute in boiling water, then drain ■ Melt 50 g (2 oz) butter or margarine in a frying pan and add the courgettes, garlic, lemon rind and lemon juice. Season and fry slowly until the courgettes are soft. Lift out the courgettes with a slotted spoon and put them aside on a plate ■ Add the remaining fat to the pan, stir in the flour and cook for 2–3 minutes. Remove from the heat and stir in the milk gradually. Bring to the boil, reduce the heat and cook for a few minutes. Beat in the soured cream and egg yolk. Cool slightly ■ Whisk the egg white stiffly, fold it into the sauce with the cheese and check the seasoning. Spread the sauce over the base of the flan case and top with the courgettes. Bake in the oven at 200°C (400°F) mark 6 for 10–15 minutes. Garnish with chives before serving.

Lining flan dish

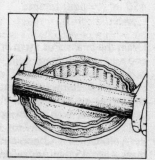

Trimming surplus pastry

Beating cream and egg yolks

VEGETABLE CURRY

Serves 4–6

1 onion, skinned and chopped
2.5-cm (1-inch) piece fresh root ginger, peeled
1–2 garlic cloves, skinned
2 fresh green chillies, seeded
30 ml (2 tbsp) oil
10 ml (2 level tsp) turmeric
10 ml (2 level tsp) coriander
10 ml (2 level tsp) cumin

8 green cardamom pods
1 cinnamon stick
1.4 kg (3 lb) mixed vegetables, including cauliflower florets, carrots, potato, parsnip, turnip and frozen peas, prepared as necessary and cut into large chunks
600 ml (1 pint) coconut milk
salt and pepper

Put the onion, ginger, garlic and chillies in a blender or food processor and purée until almost smooth ■ Heat the oil in a large, heavy-based saucepan, add the onion mixture and fry for 5 minutes, stirring constantly. Add all the spices and cook over a high heat for 3–4 minutes stirring all the time ■ Add the vegetables to the pan and stir to coat in the paste. Gradually stir in the coconut milk and 300 ml (½ pint) water. Bring to the boil, then lower the heat, cover and simmer for 45 minutes to 1 hour or until the vegetables are tender. Season and leave to stand for 5 minutes before serving.

LENTIL CASSEROLE

Serves 6

5 ml (1 level tsp) cumin seeds
15 ml (1 level tbsp) coriander seeds
5 ml (1 level tsp) mustard seeds
45 ml (3 tbsp) olive oil
350 g (12 oz) onions, skinned and sliced
450 g (1 lb) carrots, peeled and sliced
350 g (12 oz) trimmed leeks, sliced
350 g (12 oz) parsnips, peeled and chopped
2 garlic cloves, crushed

450 g (1 lb) button mushrooms, wiped and halved if large
25 g (1 oz) piece fresh root ginger, peeled and finely chopped
1.25 ml (¼ level tsp) turmeric
175 g (6 oz) split red lentils
50 g (2 oz) brown or green lentils
salt and pepper
60 ml (4 tbsp) chopped fresh coriander or parsley

Crush the cumin, coriander and mustard seeds in a mortar with a pestle or in a strong bowl with the end of a rolling pin ■ Heat the oil in a very large flameproof casserole. Add the onions, carrots, leeks and parsnips and fry for 2–3 minutes, stirring constantly. Add the garlic, mushrooms, ginger, turmeric and crushed spices, and fry for a further 2–3 minutes, stirring ■ Rinse the lentils and stir into the casserole with 750 ml (1¼ pints) boiling water. Season with salt and pepper and return to the boil. Cover and cook in the oven at 180°C (350°F) mark 4 for 45 minutes or until the vegetables and lentils are tender. Stir in the coriander or parsley and serve.

OMELETTE

Serves 1

2 eggs
10–20 ml (2–4 tsp) water

salt and pepper
15 g (1½ oz) butter

Lightly whisk together the eggs, water and some seasoning ▪ Heat the butter in a frying pan, tilting it so that the inside surface is evenly greased. Pour in the egg mixture and gently stir the mixture towards the centre with a fork, so that the uncooked egg can flow to the sides of the pan and cook ▪ Once the egg has set, stop stirring and cook the omelette for another minute, until the underside is golden brown ▪ Using a palette knife, fold one-third towards the centre, then fold the opposite third to the centre. Turn the omelette on to a warm plate, with the folded sides underneath.

Stirring mixture with fork

Folding omelette

Omelette fillings

Fines herbes Add 5 ml (1 level tsp) mixed dried herbs or 10 ml (2 tsp) finely chopped fresh herbs to the beaten egg mixture before cooking. Parsley, chives, chervil and tarragon are all suitable.

Cheese Grate 40 g (1½ oz) cheese and mix 45 ml (3 tbsp) of it with the eggs before cooking. Sprinkle the rest over the omelette after it is folded.

Tomato Skin and chop 1–2 tomatoes and fry in a little butter in a saucepan for 5 minutes, until soft and pulpy. Put in the centre of the omelette before folding.

Mushroom Wash and slice 50 g (2 oz) mushrooms and cook in butter in a saucepan until soft. Put in the centre of the omelette before folding.

Curried vegetable Roughly chop leftover vegetables, such as parsnip, potato, green beans. Fry in oil with a little crushed garlic and curry powder to taste. Put in the centre of the omelette before folding.

BAKED EGGS

Serves 4

butter or margarine
4 eggs

salt and pepper

Place small pieces of butter or margarine in individual dishes and put in the oven to melt. Break the eggs one at a time and put in the dishes. Season lightly and bake in the oven at 180°C (350°F) mark 4 for 5–8 minutes or until the eggs are just set.

EGGS FLORENTINE

Serves 4

900 g (2 lb) spinach
salt and pepper
40 g (1½ oz) butter or margarine
45 ml (3 level tbsp) plain flour

300 ml (½ pint) milk
75 g (3 oz) Cheddar cheese, grated
4 eggs

Wash the spinach well in several changes of water, put into a saucepan with a little salt and just the water that clings to the leaves. Cover and cook for 5–10 minutes, until tender. Drain well, chop roughly and reheat with a knob of butter. Melt the remaining butter, stir in the flour and cook for 2–3 minutes. Remove the pan from the heat and gradually stir in the milk; bring to the boil and continue to stir until the sauce thickens ■ Add 50 g (2 oz) cheese and season. Poach the eggs (see page 13) ■ Place the spinach in an ovenproof dish, arrange the eggs on top and pour the cheese sauce over. Sprinkle with the remaining cheese and brown under the grill.

EGGS À LA MORNAY

Serves 4

40 g (1½ oz) butter or margarine
45 ml (3 level tbsp) flour
300 ml (½ pint) milk
salt and pepper
50 g (2 oz) Cheddar cheese, grated

4 eggs, hard-boiled and sliced
chopped fresh parsley to garnish

Melt 25 g (1 oz) butter in a saucepan, stir in the flour and cook gently for 1 minute, stirring. Remove the pan from the heat and gradually stir in the milk. Bring to the boil and continue to cook, stirring until the sauce thickens. Season well and stir in 25 g (1 oz) cheese ■ Lay the eggs in an ovenproof dish, reserving a few slices to garnish. Pour over the sauce, sprinkle the remaining cheese on top and dot with the remaining butter ■ Place under a hot grill and grill   for 2–3 minutes until brown. Serve garnished with the reserved slices of egg and chopped parsley.

SAVOURY PANCAKES

Serves 4

Coating pan with batter

Turning with palette knife

Filling and rolling pancakes

125 g (4 oz) plain flour
a pinch of salt
1 egg
300 ml (½ pint) milk or
  milk and water
fat for frying

For the ratatouille filling
50 ml (2 fl oz) olive oil
2 onions, skinned and
  thinly sliced
1 large garlic clove,
  skinned and crushed
350 g (12 oz) aubergine,
  thinly sliced
450 g (1 lb) small
  courgettes, thinly sliced

450 g (1 lb) tomatoes,
  skinned, seeded and
  chopped
1 green pepper, seeded
  and chopped
1 red pepper, seeded and
  chopped
15 ml (1 tbsp) chopped
  fresh basil
10 ml (2 tsp) chopped
  fresh thyme
30 ml (2 tbsp) chopped
  fresh parsley
30 ml (2 level tbsp)
  tomato purée
salt and pepper

Make a batter by mixing the flour and salt and beating in the egg and about 30 ml (2 tbsp) milk or milk and water until smooth. Gradually beat in the remaining liquid to give a creamy batter ▪ Then make the filling. Heat the oil in a saucepan, add the onions and garlic and fry for 5 minutes until soft but not brown ▪ Add the aubergine, courgettes, tomatoes, peppers, herbs and tomato purée and seasoning. Fry for 2–3 minutes, stirring. Cover tightly and simmer for 30–40 minutes or until the vegetables are tender. Stir well. ▪ If they produce a lot of liquid, boil, uncovered, for 5–10 minutes until reduced. Taste and adjust the seasoning ▪ To make the pancakes, melt just enough fat in a thick-based frying pan and when it is hot pour in just enough batter to coat the base of the pan – about 30–45 ml (2–3 tbsp). Cook over a medium heat until brown underneath, then turn, using a palette knife, and brown the second side. Keep the pancakes hot in a warm oven and when they are all made, spread with the filling, roll up and serve at once ▪ Alternatively, place the filled pancakes in a lightly greased gratin dish, sprinkle with grated cheese, cover with foil and bake at 200°C (400°F) mark 6 for 15 minutes.

RICE AND PASTA

RICE

There are three main kinds of white rice – long, medium and short. Brown rice is available in long and short grain. It can substitute for white rice in the following recipes (except the risotto), but should be cooked for 40–45 minutes. The long slender grains are fluffy and separate when cooked and are ideal with curries and stews. Medium and short grain rice have moister, stickier grains. The medium grains are suitable for savoury dishes where the rice is moulded together. Short grain rice is used for sweet dishes. Wild rice is the seed of an aquatic grass. It is cooked like long grain rice. Mixes of long grain and wild rice are available.

BOILED RICE

Serves 3–4

225 g (8 oz) long grain white rice

5 ml (1 level tsp) salt

Place the rice in a saucepan with 600 ml (1 pint) water and salt. Bring quickly to the boil, stir well and cover ■ Reduce the heat and simmer for 14–15 minutes. Remove from the heat and separate out the grains gently. (The rice will not need draining.)

CHICKEN RISOTTO

Serves 4

75 g (3 oz) butter or margarine
2 small onions, skinned and finely chopped
1 stick celery, washed, trimmed and chopped
1 green pepper, seeded and finely chopped
50 g (2 oz) mushrooms, sliced
1 garlic clove, skinned and crushed (optional)

50 g (2 oz) bacon or ham, chopped
225 g (8 oz) long grain white rice
600 ml (1 pint) chicken stock
chopped fresh herbs as available
salt and pepper
350 g (12 oz) cooked chicken, cut into strips
grated Parmesan cheese

Melt 50 g (2 oz) butter or margarine and add the onion. Fry gently until softened. Add the celery, pepper, mushrooms, garlic and bacon or ham; fry for a few minutes, stirring ■ Add the rice and continue frying, stirring, until the rice is transparent ■ Add stock, herbs, salt and pepper. Bring to the boil, cover and simmer for 10 minutes. Add the chicken and stir well ■ Continue cooking until the rice has absorbed the liquid. Stir in the remaining butter and Parmesan and serve.

STUFFED PEPPERS

Serves 4

4 medium green peppers
40 g (1½ oz) butter or
  margarine
1 onion, skinned and
  chopped
4 tomatoes, skinned and
  chopped
100 g (4 oz) bacon,
  rinded and chopped

100 g (4 oz) long grain
  rice, cooked
salt and pepper
50 g (2 oz) Cheddar
  cheese, grated
25 g (1 oz) fresh
  breadcrumbs
150 ml (¼ pint) stock

Wipe the peppers and cut off the ends 1 cm (½ inch) below the stalk. Scoop out the seeds and core with a knife, then wash out the cases and stand them up in an ovenproof dish ■ Heat 25 g (1 oz) butter and lightly fry the onion and tomatoes; add the bacon and fry lightly. Add the cooked rice and seasoning and half the grated cheese ■ Mix the rest of the cheese with the breadcrumbs. Put the rice stuffing into the pepper cases and sprinkle with the breadcrumb mixture ■ Pour the stock round the base of the cases and cook in the oven at 190°C (375°F) mark 5 for 15–20 minutes, or until the pepper cases are cooked.

Scooping out seeds

Putting stuffing in cases

PASTA

Pasta is available plain, wholewheat, spinach (verdi), tomato, basil and garlic and can be bought fresh, raw, dried or pre-cooked dried in a variety of different shapes. The most common are described here:

Spaghetti is a thin solid rod in lengths of either 25.5 cm (10 inches) or 51 cm (20 inches). Lower it into boiling salted water and, as it softens, curve it into the pan without breaking the pieces.

Macaroni is much thicker than spaghetti and has a hole through the middle. It comes in long rods like spaghetti, or as shortcut macaroni in pieces about 2.5–4 cm (1–1½ inches) long.

Lasagne comes in flat strips 5 cm (2 inches) or 10 cm (4 inches) wide. It may be plain or green, which is flavoured with spinach.

Long noodles are narrow flat pasta in rods the same lengths as spaghetti.

Cannelloni are large tubes about 10 cm (4 inches) long, served stuffed with savoury mixtures.

Spirals, shells and other shapes are also available.

To cook pasta

Allow 50–75 g (2–3 oz) dried or 75–125 g (3–4 oz) fresh per person as a starter or accompaniment, a little more if serving as a substantial main dish. Put the pasta in a large saucepan of fast-boiling water with 5 ml (1 level tsp) salt and cook uncovered for 10–15 minutes or according to packet instructions, until the pasta is tender but still has some 'bite' in it. Drain thoroughly. Fresh pasta cooks in 2–3 minutes.

PASTA

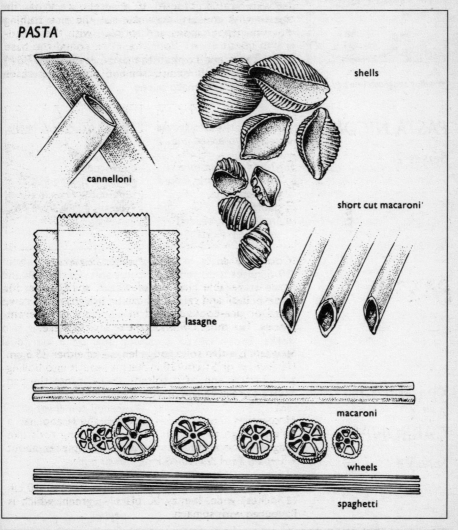

cannelloni

shells

short cut macaroni

lasagne

macaroni

wheels

spaghetti

SPAGHETTI BOLOGNESE

Serves 4

30 ml (2 tbsp) vegetable oil
1 medium onion, skinned and chopped
1 carrot, peeled and sliced
50 g (2 oz) bacon, rinded and chopped
450 g (1 lb) minced beef
226-g (8-oz) can tomatoes

50 g (2 oz) mushrooms, sliced
salt and pepper
a good dash of Worcestershire sauce
10 ml (2 level tsp) sugar
30 ml (2 tbsp) white wine or beer
350 g (12 oz) spaghetti

Winding spaghetti into pan

Put a large pan of salted water on to boil ∎ Heat the oil in a large frying pan and lightly fry the onion, carrot and bacon. Add the minced beef and fry until well browned. Add the tomatoes and mushrooms, then the seasonings and wine, and simmer for 15–20 minutes ∎ Wind the spaghetti into the pan of boiling water and boil for 10–12 minutes ∎ When the spaghetti is cooked, drain and arrange on a dish ∎ Pour the meat sauce over the spaghetti.

Note: The canned tomatoes may be replaced by 350 g (¾ lb) fresh tomatoes, skinned and chopped, or 30 ml (2 tbsp) tomato purée.

PASTA NIÇOISE

Serves 2

100 g (4 oz) pasta spirals
2 eggs, hard-boiled and shelled
113-g (4-oz) can tuna fish, drained and flaked
2 firm tomatoes, quartered
½ red pepper, seeded and finely sliced

50 g (2 oz) French beans, cooked
8 black olives
a few capers
45 ml (3 tbsp) garlic flavoured French dressing (see page 68)

Cook the pasta in boiling salted water for about 10 minutes until tender but not soft. Drain well and rinse at once in cold water. Cool ∎ Quarter the hard-boiled eggs. Place the pasta, fish, tomatoes, red pepper, beans, olives and capers in a bowl and mix gently ∎ Add French dressing and toss, using two forks. Spoon on to a serving dish or 2 individual plates. Garnish with the quartered hard-boiled eggs.

SPAGHETTI ALLA CARBONARA

Serves 4

350 g (12 oz) spaghetti
salt
2 eggs
2 egg yolks
90 ml (6 level tbsp) grated Parmesan cheese
75 g (3 oz) Cheddar cheese, grated
225 g (8 oz) streaky bacon, rinded

6 tomatoes, skinned, seeded and chopped
150 ml (¼ pint) single cream
30 ml (2 tbsp) chopped fresh parsley
50 g (2 oz) butter or margarine
freshly ground black pepper

Cook the spaghetti in fast-boiling salted water for about 10–15 minutes until tender but not soft. Drain well ■ Beat together the eggs and egg yolks, stir in half the Parmesan and half the Cheddar and set aside ■ Snip the bacon with scissors and fry without any extra fat until crisp. Stir in the chopped tomatoes ■ Reduce the heat and add the cream and parsley. Allow to simmer while the spaghetti is cooking ■ Soften the butter in the spaghetti saucepan and return the spaghetti to it. Add the bacon and cream mixture and toss well, using 2 forks. Finally add the egg mixture; toss well again. (The heat of the spaghetti is sufficient to cook the eggs.) ■ Adjust the seasoning and turn the mixture into a heated serving dish. Sprinkle the remaining cheese on top.

Draining spaghetti   *Adding egg mixture*

MACARONI CHEESE

Serves 4

175 g (6 oz) shortcut macaroni
40 g (1½ oz) butter or margarine
60 ml (4 level tbsp) plain flour

600 ml (1 pint) milk
175 g (6 oz) Cheddar cheese, grated
salt, pepper and mustard
1 tomato, sliced

Grease an ovenproof dish. Half-fill a large saucepan with water, bring to the boil and add 10 ml (2 level tsp) salt. Drop in the macaroni and cook rapidly for 10 minutes; drain well ■ Meanwhile melt the fat, stir in the flour and cook for 2–3 minutes. Remove the pan from the heat and gradually stir in the milk. Bring to the boil and continue to stir until the sauce thickens; remove from the heat and add the cheese, saving 30–45 ml (2–3 tbsp) for the topping. Season to taste with salt, pepper and mustard ■ Add the cooked macaroni to the cheese sauce and mix thoroughly. Put into the dish and sprinkle with the remaining cheese. Arrange the tomato on the top and put under a hot grill until the cheese is golden.

LASAGNE AL FORNO

Serves 4

2 × 396-g (14-oz) cans
   tomatoes
63-g (2¼-oz) can tomato
   purée
2.5–5 ml (½–1 level tsp)
   dried marjoram
salt and pepper
5 ml (1 level tsp) sugar
225 g (8 oz) cooked ham,
   diced

100 g (4 oz) lasagne
175 g (6 oz) Ricotta or
   curd cheese (or a blend
   of half cottage cheese
   and half full-fat soft
   cheese)
50 g (2 oz) grated
   Parmesan cheese
225 g (8 oz) Mozzarella
   or Bel Paese cheese

Combine the canned tomatoes, tomato purée, marjoram, seasoning and sugar, simmer gently for about 30 minutes and add the ham ■ Cook the lasagne for 10–15 minutes in boiling salted water (or as stated on the packet) and drain well ■ Cover the base of a fairly deep ovenproof dish with a layer of the tomato and meat sauce. Add half the lasagne, put in another layer of the sauce, then cover with the cheeses, using half of each kind ■ Repeat these layers with the remaining ingredients, finishing with a layer of cheese. Bake in the oven at 190°C (375°F) mark 5 for 30 minutes, until golden and bubbling on top.

Adding first layer of sauce

Adding half the lasagne

STUFFED BAKED APPLES

Serves 4

4 even-sized cooking
  apples
75–100 g (3–4 oz) mixed
  dried fruit
30 ml (2 level tbsp)
  demerara sugar

a knob of butter or
  margarine
30 ml (2 tbsp) water

Removing centre from apples

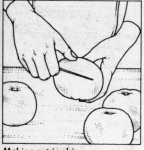

Making cut in skin

Remove the centres from the apples with a corer
and make a cut in the skin round the middle of each
apple ■ Put them in an ovenproof dish. Fill the
holes with the mixed fruit and sugar. Put a knob
of butter on each apple and pour the water round
them ■ Bake in the oven at 200°C (400°F) mark 6
for ¾–1 hour, until the apples are soft.

VARIATIONS

1 Replace the demerara sugar with golden syrup,
  honey or white sugar.
2 Include marmalade, mincemeat, chopped dates,
  almonds, walnuts or crystallised ginger in the
  filling.
3 When the apples are cooked, remove the skin
  above the cut and cover them with a meringue
  mixture made from 2 egg whites and 100 g (4 oz)
  caster sugar. Replace in the oven for a few minutes
  until lightly browned.

RHUBARB CRUMBLE

Serves 4

450 g (1 lb) rhubarb
175 g (6 oz) sugar
75 g (3 oz) butter or
  margarine

175 g (6 oz) plain flour
15 ml (1 level tbsp)
  demerara sugar for
  topping

Cut the rhubarb into pieces and put in an ovenproof
dish; add 75 g (3 oz) of the sugar ■ Rub the fat
into the flour until the texture resembles breadcrumbs. Add the remaining sugar and mix together;
sprinkle on top of the rhubarb. Finally sprinkle on
the demerara sugar and bake in the oven at 180°C
(350°F) mark 4 for 40–45 minutes ■ If you are
using a soft fruit, or one that has been already stewed,
cook the crumble at 190°C (375°F) mark 5 for about
20 minutes.

PANCAKES

Serves 4

125 g (4 oz) plain flour
a pinch of salt
1 egg
300 ml (½ pint) milk and
  water, mixed

a little lard
caster sugar
1 lemon, cut into wedges

Mix the flour and salt, make a well in the centre and break in the egg. Add half the liquid, gradually work in the flour using a wooden spoon and beat until the mixture is smooth. Add the remaining liquid gradually and beat until well mixed and the surface is covered with tiny bubbles ■ Melt just enough lard in a thick frying pan to coat the bottom and sides, then pour off any surplus. When the fat is hot, pour in a little batter – just enough to cover the bottom of the pan ■ Cook the pancake until it is golden brown on the underside, then toss or turn it over and cook the other side ■ Turn out on to a plate, sprinkle with sugar, cover with another plate and keep warm whilst the rest are being made ■ When all the pancakes are cooked roll them up singly and serve with wedges of lemon.

Turning pancake

Serving

APPLE PIE

Serves 4

200 g (7 oz) shortcrust
  pastry (see page 104)
450 g (1 lb) cooking
  apples, peeled and
  sliced

100g (4 oz) demerara
  sugar
4 cloves
egg or milk to glaze

Lining bottom of pie plate

Putting on lid

Roll out half the pastry and line the bottom of an 18-cm (7-inch) pie plate ■ Fill the plate with the sliced apples, sprinkle with the sugar and add the cloves ■ Roll out the remaining half of the pastry to make the top crust of the pie. Brush the edge of the bottom layer of pastry with water, put on the lid and seal well. Mark the edges with a knife and crimp together. Brush with beaten egg or milk ■ Bake in the oven at 200°C (400°F) mark 6 for 15–20 minutes, then lower the temperature to 180°C (350°F) mark 4 and cook for a further 15–20 minutes, or until the apple is cooked (test with a thin skewer).

BANANAS WITH HONEY AND ORANGE

Serves 4

25 g (1 oz) butter
45 ml (3 tbsp) clear
  honey
2.5 ml (½ level tsp)
  mixed spice

grated rind of 1 orange
juice of 2 oranges
4 medium bananas,
  peeled and halved
  lengthways

Melt the butter and honey in a large frying pan and add the spice, orange rind and juice ■ Place the banana halves in the syrup and gently poach for 5 minutes ■ Serve hot with whipped cream.

BAKED JAM SPONGE

Serves 3–4

75 g (3 oz) butter or
  margarine
75 g (3 oz) caster sugar
1 egg, beaten
150 g (5 oz) self-raising
  flour

2.5 ml (½ tsp) vanilla
  flavouring
milk to mix
30–45 ml (2–3 tbsp) jam

Grease a 600–900-ml (1–1½-pint) pie dish ■ Cream the fat and sugar until pale and fluffy. Add the egg a little at a time, beating after each addition. Fold in the flour with the flavouring and a little milk to give a dropping consistency ■ Put the jam in a layer in the base of the prepared dish and spoon in the sponge mixture ■ Bake in the oven at 180°C (350°F) mark 4 for 30–40 minutes, until well risen and golden. Serve with a custard sauce.

Creaming fat and sugar

Putting jam in dish

LEMON MERINGUE PIE

serves 4

shortcrust pastry made
   with 150 g (5 oz) flour
   (see page 104)
45 ml (3 level tbsp)
   cornflour
150 ml (¼ pint) water
juice and grated rind of 2
   lemons

100 g (4 oz) sugar
2 eggs, separated
100 g (4 oz) caster sugar
glacé cherries and
   angelica

Roll out the pastry and use it to line an 18-cm (7-inch) flan case or deep pie plate. Trim the edges and bake blind (see page 106) in the oven at 220°C (425°F) mark 7 for 15 minutes. Remove the paper and baking beans and return the case to the oven for a further 5 minutes. Reduce the oven temperature to 180°C (350°F) mark 4 ■ Mix the cornflour with the water in a saucepan, add the lemon juice and rind and bring slowly to the boil, stirring until the mixture thickens, then add the sugar. Remove from the heat, cool the mixture slightly and add the egg yolks. Pour into the pastry case ■ Whisk the egg whites until stiff, whisk in half the caster sugar and fold in the rest. Pile the meringue on top of the lemon filling and bake in the oven for about 10 minutes, or until the meringue is crisp and lightly browned. Decorate before serving with cherries and angelica.

Stirring until mixture thickens

Whisking in half sugar

Spooning meringue on filling

CHRISTMAS PUDDINGS

175 g (6 oz) almonds
550 g (1¼ lb) seedless
   raisins
350 g (12 oz) currants
225 g (8 oz) sultanas
100 g (4 oz) mixed peel
100 g (4 oz) glacé cherries
225 g (8 oz) cooking
   apples, peeled and cored
grated rind and juice of
   1 lemon and 1 orange
350 g (12 oz) plain flour
5 ml (1 level tsp) salt

10 ml (2 level tsp) mixed
   spice
350 g (12 oz) fresh
   breadcrumbs
350 g (12 oz) shredded
   suet
225 g (8 oz) caster sugar
225 g (8 oz) soft brown
   sugar
60 ml (4 tbsp) brandy
4 eggs
about 150 ml (¼ pint)
   milk

Grease 3 pudding basins – 600-ml, 900-ml, 1.1-litre (1-pint, 1½-pint and 2-pint). Blanch the almonds, remove the skins when cool, then dry the nuts. Wash and dry the fruit thoroughly, or rub it in flour on a sieve to remove any small stalks, etc. Chop the nuts, peel, cherries and apple and mix with the diced fruit and the lemon and orange rind. Add the mixture to the flour, salt, spice, breadcrumbs, suet and sugars ■ Mix together the fruit juices, brandy and eggs and mix very thoroughly with the dry ingredients, adding enough milk to give a dropping consistency ■ Turn the mixture into the prepared basins and cover with greaseproof paper and a pudding cloth or foil secured with string. Either steam or boil in a saucepan with water coming halfway up the basins. Top up the basins with boiling water as necessary. Allow the following times:

600-ml (1-pint) pudding – about 5 hours
900-ml (1½-pint) pudding – about 7 hours
1.1-litre (2-pint) pudding – about 9 hours.

When the puddings are cool, remove the pudding cloths and replace with new ones ■ The puddings will keep in a cool place for 4 months. Before serving, cook again for the following times:

600-ml (1-pint) pudding – 2 hours
900-ml (1½-pint) pudding – 3 hours
1.1-litre (2-pint) pudding – 3 hours.

Removing skins from almonds

Rubbing fruit in flour

Grating lemon

Securing pudding cloth

STEWED PLUMS

Serves 4

450 g (1 lb) plums
50–75 g (2–3 oz) sugar

300 ml (½ pint) water

Halve and stone the plums, reserving the stones. Crack the stones with nutcrackers and remove the kernels; reserve ■ Make a syrup by dissolving the sugar in the water over a gentle heat. Add the plums and the kernels and simmer gently until the fruit is soft but keeps its shape ■ Remove the kernels with a slotted spoon before serving.

MINCE PIES

Makes about 20

shortcrust pastry made
  with 350 g (12 oz) flour
  (see page 104)
350–450 g (¾–1 lb)
  mincemeat

milk or egg to glaze
caster sugar for dusting

Filling with mincemeat

Roll out the pastry to a 3-mm (⅛-inch) thickness. Cut into about 20 rounds with a 7.5-cm (3-inch) fluted cutter and 20 smaller rounds with a 5.5-cm (2¼-inch) cutter ■ Line 6.5-cm (2½-inch) patty tins with the larger rounds and fill with mincemeat. Damp the edges of the small rounds and place firmly in position on top of the pies ■ Make a small slit in the top of each pie, brush with milk or egg and bake in the oven at 220°C (425°F) mark 7 for 15–20 minutes, until light golden brown. Cool on a wire rack ■ Reheat and dust with caster sugar before serving.

APPLE AND BLACKBERRY CHARLOTTE

Serves 4

450 g (1 lb) cooking
  apples, peeled
450 g (1 lb) blackberries
grated rind and juice of
  ½ a lemon
1.25 ml (¼ level tsp)
  ground cinnamon

50 g (2 oz) butter, melted
6 slices bread from a
  large white loaf, crusts
  removed
125–175 g (4–6 oz) sugar
30 ml (2 level tbsp) bread
  or cake crumbs

Quarter the apples and remove the cores; wash and pick over the blackberries. Stew the fruit in a pan with the lemon rind and juice and the cinnamon ■ Brush a charlotte mould or a 12.5-cm (5-inch) cake tin generously with melted butter ■ Trim one piece of bread to a round the same size as the base of the tin, dip it in melted butter and fit it into the bottom of the tin. Dip the remaining slices of bread in the butter and arrange closely around the sides of the tin, reserving one piece for the top ■ Add the sugar and crumbs to the stewed fruit, mix well and fill the tin. Cover with the remaining slice of bread, trimmed to fit the top of the mould ■ Cook in the oven at 190°C (375°F) mark 5 for about 1 hour, turn out and serve with custard or cream.

Fitting bread in bottom of tin

Arranging slices round sides

Covering with slice of bread

COLD PUDDINGS

APRICOT FOOL

Serves 4

439-g (15½-oz) can apricots
150 ml (¼ pint) custard
150 ml (¼ pint) double cream

chopped walnuts (optional)

Drain the apricots and purée in a blender or rub through a sieve. Add this pulp to the custard. Lightly whip the cream and fold into the mixture. Pile into glasses and decorate the top with chopped nuts, if used.

Fruit fool is an adaptable sweet that can be made from many types of fruit, though those with a strong flavour taste best, eg rhubarb, damsons, raspberries, blackberries and perhaps the most traditional of all, gooseberries.
For a more economical version, use all custard – for a richer flavour increase the proportion of cream; the authentic old English recipe uses all cream, giving a gorgeous rich sweet.
Serve something crisp with fruit fool as a contrast to its smooth texture – for instance, plain sweet biscuits or sponge fingers.

RASPBERRY MOUSSE

Serves 4

450 g (1 lb) raspberries, fresh or frozen and thawed
caster sugar to taste
150 ml (¼ pint) double or whipping cream, whipped

45 ml (3 tbsp) water or juice from the canned raspberries
20 ml (4 level tsp) gelatine
2 egg whites
whipped cream to decorate

Sieve the raspberries, to make about 300 ml (½ pint) purée. Stir in sugar to taste and the whipped cream. Put the water or fruit juice in a small basin and sprinkle the gelatine on it, leave to stand for about 10 minutes or until sponge-like in texture, then stand the basin in a pan of hot water and heat gently until the gelatine is dissolved; allow to cool slightly ■ Pour the gelatine into the raspberry cream in a steady stream, stirring the mixture all the time ■ Whisk the egg whites until stiff and fold them into the raspberry cream, using a large metal spoon. Pour the mousse into a serving dish and chill until set. Decorate with whipped cream before serving.

CHOCOLATE MOUSSE

Serves 4

175 g (6 oz) plain
  chocolate
3 eggs, separated
150 ml (¼ pint) double
  cream, whipped

grated chocolate or finely
  chopped nuts

Melt the chocolate in a bowl over a pan of hot water.
Remove from the heat then beat the yolks into the
melted chocolate ▪ Whisk the whites until stiff
and carefully fold into the chocolate mixture ▪
Chill and serve in individual ramekin dishes or small
sundae glasses, topped with whipped cream and
grated chocolate or chopped nuts.

TO MELT CHOCOLATE

Break up the chocolate and place the pieces in a
heatproof bowl which will fit over a saucepan. Half
fill the saucepan with water and stand over a low
heat. Stir the chocolate until it melts.

FRUIT TRIFLE

Serves 4

6 individual sponge cakes
raspberry jam
1 glass sherry or fruit
  juice
2 bananas, sliced

2 peaches, sliced
450 ml (¾ pint) custard
150 ml (¼ pint) double
  cream
chocolate vermicelli

Split the sponge cakes, spread with jam, cut into small
pieces and place in the bottom of a large bowl ▪
Pour the sherry or fruit juice over and leave to soak
for 30 minutes ▪ Cover the cake with the mixed
fruits. Pour the custard over the cake and fruit and
allow to set ▪ Whip the cream lightly, spread over
the top and sprinkle chocolate vermicelli round the
edge.

FRUIT FLANS

shortcrust flan case,
  baked blind (see page
  106)

For fresh fruit filling
225 g (8 oz) fresh fruit,
  eg raspberries,
  strawberries
30–45 ml (2–3 tbsp)
  redcurrant jelly or
  apricot jam, sieved

For canned fruit filling
425-g (15-oz) can fruit
15 ml (1 level tbsp)
  cornflour
150 ml (¼ pint) fruit
  juice

For a fresh fruit flan, pick over the fruit, wash it and
arrange in the flan case ▪ Make a glaze by melting
the redcurrant jelly or apricot jam with about 15 ml
(1 tbsp) water. Cool until it begins to thicken, then
brush the glaze over the fruit. Leave to set before

serving ■ For a canned fruit flan, arrange the drained fruit in the flan case, filling it well. Blend the cornflour with a little of the fruit juice to a smooth cream. Boil the rest of the juice and stir into the blended cornflour. Return this mixture to the pan and bring to the boil, stirring until a thickened glaze is obtained. Spoon over the fruit to coat it evenly ■ In each case, adapt the quantity of fruit to suit the size of the flan case.

LEMON CHEESECAKE

Serves 8

1½ packets of lemon jelly
60 ml (4 tbsp) water
2 eggs, separated
300 ml (½ pint) milk
grated rind of 2 lemons
90 ml (6 tbsp) lemon juice
450 g (1 lb) cottage cheese
15 ml (1 level tbsp) caster sugar
150 ml (¼ pint) double cream, whipped

For the crumb base
100 g (4 oz) digestive biscuits
50 g (2 oz) caster sugar
50 g (2 oz) butter or margarine, melted

For the decoration
glacé cherries and mint sprigs

Put the jelly and water in a small pan and warm gently over a low heat, stirring until dissolved ■ Beat together the egg yolks and milk, pour on to the jelly, stir and return the mixture to the heat for a few minutes without boiling. Remove from the heat and add the lemon rind and juice ■ Sieve the cottage cheese and stir it into the jelly, or put both jelly and cottage cheese in a blender and purée until smooth. Turn the mixture into a bowl ■ Whisk the egg whites until stiff, add the caster sugar and whisk again until stiff; fold into the cheese mixture. Fold in the whipped cream and spoon the mixture into a 20.5-cm (8-inch) spring release cake tin fitted with a loose base ■ Crush the biscuits and stir in the sugar and butter. Use to cover the cheese mixture, pressing it on lightly; chill ■ Turn the cheesecake out carefully inverting it on to a serving plate and decorate with cherries and mint sprigs.

Sieving cottage cheese

Crushing biscuits

Covering cheese mixture

SUMMER PUDDING

Serves 4

150 g (5 oz) sugar
30 ml (2 tbsp) water
450 g (1 lb) mixed
    blackcurrants,
    redcurrants and
    raspberries, washed

100–175 g (4–6 oz)
    white bread, cut in thin
    slices
whipped cream or crème
    fraîche

Stir the sugar and water together in a saucepan and bring slowly to the boil. Add the fruits and stew gently until they are soft but retain their shape ■ Cut the crusts from the bread and line a 900-ml (1½-pint) pudding basin with the slices ■ Pour in the fruit and cover with more slices of bread. Place a saucer with a weight on it on top of the pudding and leave overnight in a cool place ■ Turn out the pudding and serve with whipped cream or crème fraîche ■ Other soft fruits (or a mixture) may be used, providing they have a rich, strong colour – for example loganberries, blueberries, damsons. A proportion of apple can also be included.

Lining pudding basin with bread

Weighting down pudding

Turning out pudding

STRAWBERRY SHORTCAKE

Serves 4–6

225 g (8 oz) self-raising
    flour
pinch of salt
100 g (4 oz) butter or
    margarine
75 g (3 oz) sugar
1 egg, beaten

15–30 ml (1–2 tbsp) milk
350–450 g (¾–1 lb)
    strawberries
45–60 ml (3–4 level tbsp)
    caster sugar
150 ml (¼ pint) double
    cream

Grease a 20.5-cm (8-inch) sandwich cake tin ■ Sift the flour and salt together and rub in the fat until the mixture resembles breadcrumbs; stir in the sugar. Add the egg a little at a time and a little milk, so that the mixture begins to stick together ■ Collect the mixture together with the hand and knead lightly into a smooth, fairly firm dough. Turn on to a floured board and roll out the dough into a round 20.5 cm (8 inches) across ■ Press the dough evenly into the cake tin and bake in the oven at 190°C (375°F) mark 5 for 20 minutes, or until golden and firm. Turn out of the tin on to a cooling tray ■ Wash the strawberries and set aside about 12 for decorating; lightly crush the rest and sprinkle with 30–45 ml (2–3 tbsp) caster sugar ■ Split the shortcake, spread the lower half with the crushed fruit and replace the top. Add the remaining sugar to the cream and pile on the cake. Decorate with the whole berries.

Rolling out dough

Splitting shortcake

Decorating with whole berries

CRÈME CARAMEL

Serves 4–6

115 g (4½ oz) sugar
150 ml (¼ pint) water

600 ml (1 pint) milk
4 eggs

Put 100 g (4 oz) of the sugar and the water into a small pan and dissolve the sugar slowly; bring to the boil and boil without stirring until it forms a rich golden brown caramel ■ Pour into a warmed 15-cm (6-inch) cake tin, turning the tin until the bottom is completely covered. (Take care as it will be very hot.) ■ Warm the milk, pour on to the lightly whisked eggs and remaining sugar and strain over the cooled caramel ■ Place the tin in a shallow tin of water and bake in the oven at 170°C (325°F) mark 3 for 1 hour, until set ■ Leave in the tin until quite cold (preferably until the next day) before turning out ■ Individual crèmes are easier to turn out. Divide the mixture between six 150-ml (¼-pint) caramel coated tins or ramekin dishes. Cook for about 45 minutes.

Pouring on milk

Placing tin in tin of water

SORBETS

For each of the following sorbets you will need 350 ml (12 fl oz) sugar syrup. To make this, put 125 g (4 oz) granulated sugar in a heavy-based saucepan. Add 300 ml (½ pint) water and heat gently until the sugar dissolves. Do not stir the ingredients but occasionally loosen the sugar from the base of the pan to help it dissolve. Boil for 2 minutes. Cool.

LEMON SORBET

Serves 3–4

350 ml (12 fl oz) sugar syrup (see above)

finely pared rind and juice of 3 lemons
1 egg white

Prepare the sugar syrup as far as dissolving the sugar. Add the pared lemon rinds and simmer gently for about 10 minutes. Leave to cool completely ■ Stir in the lemon juice and strain into a shallow non-metal, freezerproof container. Cover and freeze for about 3 hours until mushy ■ Whisk the egg white until stiff. Turn the sorbet into a bowl and beat gently to break down the ice crystals. Fold in the egg white ■ Return to the container, cover and freeze for 4 hours or until firm. Transfer to the refrigerator about 40 minutes before serving to soften slightly

VARIATIONS

Orange – Replace the lemons with the pared rind and juice of 2 oranges.
Lime – Replace the lemons with the pared rind and juice of 5 limes.

RASPBERRY SORBET

Serves 6

450 g (1 lb) raspberries
30 ml (2 tbsp) lemon juice
30 ml (2 tbsp) kirsch

350 ml (12 fl oz) sugar syrup (see above)
2 egg whites

Purée the raspberries with the lemon juice and kirsch in a blender or food processor. Press through a nylon sieve, and add to the sugar syrup ■ Freeze as for Lemon Sorbet, adding the egg whites as directed. Transfer to the refrigerator about 30 minutes before serving to soften slightly.

MANGO SORBET

Serves 8

2 large ripe mangoes, peeled
juice of 1 large lime

350 ml (12 fl oz) sugar syrup (see above)
1 egg white

Purée the mango flesh in a blender or food processor. Press through a sieve. Mix with the lime juice and sugar syrup ■ Freeze as for Lemon Sorbet, adding the egg white as directed. Serve straight from the freezer.

VANILLA ICE CREAM

Serves 4–6

1 vanilla pod, split, or
  2.5 ml (½ tsp) vanilla
  essence
300 ml (½ pint) milk
3 egg yolks

50–75 g (2–3 oz) caster
  sugar
300 ml (½ pint) double
  cream

Put the milk and vanilla pod in a heavy-based saucepan and bring almost to the boil. Remove from the heat, cover and leave to infuse for about 20 minutes ■ Beat the egg yolks and sugar together in a bowl until well blended. Stir in the milk and strain back into the pan. Cook the custard over a gentle heat, stirring all the time, until it thickens just enough to lightly coat the back of the spoon. Do not boil or it will curdle. Pour into a bowl and leave to cool ■ Whisk the cream into the cold custard mixture, with the vanilla essence, if using ■ Turn into a shallow freeezerproof container and freeze for about 3 hours until mushy ■ Turn into a bowl and beat with a fork to break down the ice crystals ■ Return to the freezer for about 2 hours, then beat again. Freeze until firm ■ Alternatively, freeze in an ice cream machine. Leave at cool room temperature for 20–30 minutes to soften before serving.

Whisking cream until thick

Turning mixture into freezing tray

VARIATIONS

Fruit – Add 300 ml (½ pint) fruit purée, sweetened to taste, to the cooled custard.

Chocolate – Gently heat the milk in a pan with 125 g (4 oz) plain chocolate until the chocolate melts, then cook over a high heat until almost boiling. Continue as above.

Chocolate flake – Crumble 2 large chocolate flakes. Stir half into the cooled custard with the cream. Continue as above. Stir in remaining flake just before the ice cream freezes.

Coffee – Add 150 ml (¼ pint) cold strong fresh coffee to the cooled custard or 10 ml (2 tsp) instant coffee granules instead of the milk or the vanilla pod.

Coconut – Finely chop 175 g (6 oz) creamed coconut. Add to the milk and warm until dissolved, whisking until smooth, then add 30 ml (2 tbsp) lemon juice. Complete as above, omitting the vanilla.

SAUCES, STUFFINGS AND ACCOMPANIMENTS

WHITE SAUCE

20 g (³/₄ oz) butter or
  margarine
30 ml (2 level tbsp) plain
  flour

300 ml (½ pint) milk
salt and pepper

Melt the fat in a small saucepan, add the flour and stir well with a wooden spoon until smooth. Cook for 2–3 minutes then remove it from the heat ■ Add the milk a little at a time, stirring thoroughly before adding any more. Return the sauce to the heat and bring to the boil, stirring all the time, until it thickens. Cook for a further 1–2 minutes. Season to taste ■ For a coating sauce use 25 g (1 oz) each of fat and flour to 300 ml (½ pint) milk.

Melting fat in saucepan

Adding flour and stirring

Adding milk

VARIATIONS

Use a base of 300 ml (½ pint) white sauce.

Parsley Add 30 ml (2 tbsp) chopped parsley. If the sauce is to accompany fish, add a little lemon juice or vinegar; stir thoroughly and reheat.

Cheese To the hot sauce add 50–75 g (2–3 oz) grated cheese, a little mustard and a few drops of Worcestershire sauce.

Onion Skin and chop 1–2 onions and cook in just enough water to cover until tender. Use 150 ml (¼ pint) cooking liquid and 150 ml (¼ pint) milk to make the sauce, then add the onion.

Egg Add 1–2 finely chopped hard-boiled eggs.

Anchovy Omit the salt. Add 15–30 ml (1–2 tbsp) anchovy essence to taste and a drop or two of pink colouring to tint.

Mushroom Add 50 g (2 oz) sliced sautéed button mushrooms and cook for 2–3 minutes.

Shrimp Add 25–50 g (1–2 oz) chopped shrimps (or prawns), with a little lemon juice and anchovy essence.

Caper Add 25–50 g (1–2 oz) capers (chopped or whole) and a little of the liquid or some lemon juice.

BREAD SAUCE

a few cloves
1 onion, skinned
450 ml (¾ pint) milk
75 g (3 oz) fresh
  breadcrumbs

a knob of butter
salt and pepper

Stick the cloves into the onion, put in a saucepan with the milk and bring almost to the boil; leave for 20 minutes ■ Add the crumbs and butter and season to taste. Remove the onion and reheat.

MINT SAUCE

a small bunch of fresh
  mint
10 ml (2 level tsp) sugar
15 ml (1 tbsp) boiling

water
30 ml (2 tbsp) vinegar

Wash the mint and strip the leaves from the stalks; chop as finely as possible ■ Put the sugar into a sauceboat, pour on the boiling water, stir until dissolved, then add the chopped mint and vinegar.

Chopping mint finely   Adding vinegar

GRAVY

A rich brown gravy is served with all roast joints. There should be no need to use extra colouring or flavouring if the gravy is properly made in the baking tin after the joint has been removed.

To make thin gravy, pour the fat very slowly from the tin, draining it off carefully from one corner and leaving the sediment behind. Season well with salt and pepper and add 300 ml (½ pint) hot vegetable water or stock (which can be made from a bouillon cube). Stir thoroughly until all the sediment is scraped from the tin and the gravy is a rich brown; return the pan to the heat and boil for 2–3 minutes. Serve very hot.

To make a thick gravy, leave 30 ml (2 tbsp) of the fat in the tin, add 30 ml (2 level tbsp) flour (if this is shaken from a flour dredger it gives a smoother result), blend well and cook over the heat until it turns brown, stirring continuously. Carefully mix in 300 ml (½ pint) hot stock, boil for 2–3 minutes, season well, strain and serve very hot.

Greasy gravy, due to not draining off enough fat, should be skimmed before use. If the gravy is too thin, boil down the liquid to reduce slightly. If the sauce is very pale, extra colouring can be added in the form of gravy browning. Meat extracts, which are sometimes added to give extra taste, overpower the characteristic meat flavour. However, a sliced carrot and onion cooked with the joint in the gravy will give extra 'body' to the taste without impairing it; 15 ml (1 tbsp) cider or wine added at the last moment does wonders.

BARBECUE SAUCE

Serves 4

50 g (2 oz) butter
1 large onion, skinned and chopped
5 ml (1 level tsp) tomato purée
30 ml (2 tbsp) vinegar
30 ml (2 level tbsp) demerara sugar

10 ml (2 level tsp) dry mustard
30 ml (2 tbsp) Worcestershire sauce
150 ml (¼ pint) water

Melt the butter and fry the onion for 5 minutes or until soft. Stir in the tomato purée and continue cooking for a further 3 minutes ■ Blend the remaining ingredients to a smooth cream and stir in the onion mixture ■ Return the sauce to the pan and simmer uncovered for a further 10 minutes ■ Serve with chicken, sausages, hamburgers or chops.

TOMATO SAUCE

Makes about
450 ml (¾ pint)

½ onion, skinned and
  chopped
2 rashers of bacon, rinded
  and chopped
a knob of butter
25 ml (1½ level tbsp)
  plain flour
396-g (14-oz) can tomatoes

1 clove
½ bay leaf
few sprigs of rosemary, or
  5 ml (1 level tsp) dried
  mixed herbs
a pinch of sugar
salt and pepper

Fry the onion and bacon gently in the butter for 5 minutes ■ Stir in the flour and gradually add the tomatoes with their juice, also the flavourings and seasoning ■ Simmer gently for 15 minutes, then sieve and check the seasoning ■ Serve with croquettes, pasta and other savoury dishes.

EGG CUSTARD SAUCE

Makes about
300 ml (½ pint)

1 whole egg plus 1 egg
  yolk or 3 yolks
15 ml (1 level tbsp) sugar
300 ml (½ pint) milk

few strips of thinly pared
  lemon rind or ½ vanilla
  pod, split

Whisk the eggs or yolks and sugar lightly. Warm the milk and lemon rind or vanilla pod and leave for 10 minutes for the flavour to infuse ■ Pour the milk on to the eggs then strain the mixture into the top of a double saucepan or into a thick-based saucepan. Stir over a very gentle heat until the sauce thickens and lightly coats the back of the spoon. Do not let it boil or it will curdle ■ Serve hot or cold with fruit sweets and puddings.

Pouring the milk on to the eggs

BRANDY BUTTER

Serves 4–6

75 g (3 oz) butter
75 g (3 oz) caster sugar

10–15 ml (2–3 tsp)
  brandy

Cream the butter until pale and soft. Beat in the sugar gradually, then add the brandy a few drops at a time, taking care not to allow the mixture to curdle. The finished sauce should be pale and frothy. Pile it into a small dish and leave to harden before serving with Christmas pudding.

APPLE SAUCE

Serves 4

450 g (1 lb) cooking apples, peeled and cored

25 g (1 oz) butter
a little sugar

Slice the apples and simmer in an open saucepan with 30–45 ml (2–3 tbsp) water until soft and thick — about 10 minutes ■ Beat to a pulp with a wooden spoon or potato masher then purée in a blender or rub through a sieve if you wish ■ Stir in the butter and add a little sugar if the apples are very tart ■ Serve with pork or sausages.

FORCEMEAT

100 g (4 oz) fresh breadcrumbs
25–50 g (1–2 oz) bacon or ham, chopped
15 ml (1 level tbsp) chopped fresh parsley

50 g (2 oz) suet
grated rind of ¼ a lemon
2.5 ml (½ level tsp) mixed herbs
salt and pepper
beaten egg

Mix all the ingredients together with a little beaten egg until the stuffing binds well ■ Use with meat, poultry, fish and liver. Sufficient for an average-sized joint or chicken.

SAGE AND ONION STUFFING

2 large onions, skinned
25 g (1 oz) butter or margarine
100 g (4 oz) fresh breadcrumbs

10 ml (2 level tsp) dried sage
salt and pepper

Chop the onions finely. Melt the butter and fry the onions until tender. Combine with the remaining ingredients and mix well ■ Use with roast goose, duck and pork.

SAUSAGE STUFFING

1 large onion, skinned and chopped
450 g (1 lb) pork sausagemeat
25 g (1 oz) butter or margarine
10 ml (2 level tsp) chopped fresh parsley

5 ml (1 level tsp) mixed herbs
25 g (1 oz) fresh breadcrumbs (optional)
salt and pepper

Mix the onion with the sausagemeat. Melt the butter and fry the sausagemeat and onion lightly for 2–3 minutes. Add the rest of the ingredients and mix well ■ Use with chicken and turkey. Sufficient for a 4.5 kg (10 lb) turkey.

YORKSHIRE PUDDING

Serves 4

125 g (4 oz) plain flour
a pinch of salt
1 egg, beaten

300 ml (½ pint) milk and
   water mixed
dripping or oil

Sift the flour and salt into a mixing bowl and make a well in the centre. Pour the egg and 30 ml (2 tbsp) of the liquid into the well ■ Using a wooden spoon and working from the centre, gradually mix some of the flour from the edges into the egg and milk and beat well until smooth ■ Gradually add 150 ml (¼ pint) of the liquid, beating gently and drawing in the rest of the flour until all is mixed in and the batter is smooth and bubbly. Stir in the remaining liquid. Put a little dripping or oil into a shallow tin measuring about 18 cm (7 inches) square and heat in the oven. Pour in the batter and bake in the oven at 220°C (425°F) mark 7 for 40–45 minutes. Cut into squares and serve with roast beef.

Pouring egg and liquid in well   *Pouring batter in shallow tin*

POPOVERS

Makes about 12

Make the batter as for Yorkshire pudding. Heat the oven to 220°C (425°F) mark 7. Put a little lard or dripping or oil into some deep patty tins, heat in the oven, then pour some batter into each tin. Bake near the top of the oven for 15–20 minutes. Serve with roast beef.

Pouring batter in patty tins

PASTRY

Plain flour is usually recommended for making pastry;
if self-raising is used, it gives a more open and spongy
texture. A variety of fats (including butter, margarine
and lard, or a combination) can be used for shortcrust, but for richer pastries it is better to use the fat
recommended in the particular recipe. Proprietary
vegetable shortenings are excellent; follow the
makers' directions, as they sometimes advise using
less fat to flour than in standard recipes.
Avoid using too much flour on board and rolling pin,
as this alters the proportions. Take care also with the
liquid — too much makes the pastry tough.

Note: '200 g (7 oz) pastry' means pastry made with
200 g (7 oz) flour and other ingredients in proportion. With ready-made pastries, the amount refers to
the total weight, as bought.

SHORTCRUST PASTRY

200 g (7 oz) plain flour
2.5 ml (½ level tsp) salt
100 g (3½ oz) butter or
  margarine

about 35 ml (7 tsp) cold
  water

Sifting flour and salt

Sift the flour and salt into a basin ▪ Cut the fat
into the flour and complete the mixing by rubbing in
with the fingertips, until no lumps of fat remain ▪
Add just enough cold water to bind the mixture,
mixing with a round-bladed knife until it is evenly distributed ▪ Draw the pastry together with the
fingertips to form a stiff dough; knead lightly until
smooth ▪ Turn it on to a lightly floured board and
roll out and use as required.

Rubbing in with fingertips

Adding cold water

Drawing pastry together

WHOLEMEAL PASTRY

Follow the recipe for shortcrust pastry, using wholemeal flour instead of white flour. Add a little extra water.

FLAKY PASTRY

200 g (7 oz) plain white
  flour
a pinch of salt
150 g (5 oz) butter, or
  block margarine

about 105 ml (7 tbsp)
  cold water to mix
squeeze of lemon juice
beaten egg to glaze

Sift together the flour and salt ■ Soften the fat by 'working' it with a knife on a plate and divide it into 4 equal portions ■ Rub one-quarter of the fat into the flour and mix to a soft elastic dough with the water and lemon juice ■ On a floured board, roll the pastry to an oblong 3 times as long as it is wide ■ Put another quarter of the fat over the top two-thirds of the pastry in flakes, so that it looks like buttons on a card ■ Fold the bottom third up and the top third of the pastry down and turn it through 90° so that the folds are now at the side ■ Seal the edges of the pastry by pressing with the rolling pin. Re-roll as before and continue until all the fat is used up ■ Wrap the pastry loosely in greaseproof paper and leave it to 'rest' in the refrigerator for at least 30 minutes before using ■ Roll it out on a lightly floured board to a 3-mm (⅛-inch) thickness and use as required. Brush with beaten egg before baking to give the characteristic glaze.

Putting fat on pastry in flakes

Folding bottom third up

Sealing edges of pastry

SUETCRUST PASTRY

200 g (7 oz) self-raising flour
5 ml (1 level tsp) salt
100 g (3½ oz) shredded suet

about 105–120 ml (7–8 tbsp) water

Mix together the flour, salt and suet. Add enough cold water to give a light elastic dough and knead very lightly until smooth. Roll out to a 5-mm (¼-inch) thickness ■ This pastry may be used for both sweet and savoury dishes and can be steamed, boiled or baked; the first two are the most satisfactory methods, as baked suetcrust pastry is inclined to be hard.

MAKING A FLAN CASE

Turn the pastry on to a board and roll out a circle about 5 cm (2 inches) wider than the flan case, ring or tin. With the rolling pin, lift the pastry and lower it into the case. Lightly press the pastry into the case then turn any surplus pastry outwards over the rim. Roll across the top with the rolling pin to trim the edges. Bake blind as described below.

Filling case with dried beans

Removing beans and paper

BAKING BLIND

Baking blind is the term used to describe cooking a pastry case or shell without a filling. To keep the case a good shape, cover the surface of the uncooked pastry with a large piece of foil or greaseproof paper, then fill with some dried beans or peas kept specially for this purpose. Bake at 200°C (400°F) mark 6 for 15 minutes. Remove the beans and paper and return the flan case to the oven for about 5 minutes to allow the pastry to dry out. Remove from the oven and cool.

Pastry cases which have been baked blind may be stored in a tin when cold and kept until required. Fill them with fruit or any suitable sweet or savoury mixture and garnish or decorate.

CAKES AND BISCUITS

LINING CAKE TINS

Grease the tin by brushing with oil or melted vegetable fat. Stand the tin on a sheet of greaseproof paper and draw round it with a pencil. Cut out the shape just inside the pencilled line. Measure the depth of the tin and add an extra 5 cm (2 inches); now cut a strip of greaseproof paper this width and long enough to encircle the tin. It may be necessary to cut 2 strips to give the right length. Turn up 1 cm (½ inch) along one long edge of the strip and make slanting cuts at 1-cm (½-inch) intervals, going as far as the crease. Fit the strips neatly into place round the sides of the tin, with the snipped edge on the base. Fit the base paper into the bottom. Finally, brush all the lining paper with oil or melted fat.

With a shallow sandwich tin it is normal to line the base only, with a circle of paper that fits exactly.

Fitting paper in round tin   Fitting paper in square tin

With a rich fruit cake, double greaseproof paper should be used to prevent overbrowning and drying of the outside crust. When cooking a Christmas cake wrap an extra layer of brown paper or newspaper round the outside of the tin.

If you notice that a cake is browning too quickly on top, place a piece of paper over it for the second half of the cooking time.

Non-stick baking parchment does not need greasing. As an extra precaution, it is safest to base-line non-stick tins.

VICTORIA SANDWICH

100 g (4 oz) butter or margarine
100 g (4 oz) caster sugar
2 eggs, beaten

100 g (4 oz) self-raising flour, sifted
30–45 ml (2–3 tbsp) jam
caster sugar to dredge

Grease and base-line with greased greaseproof paper two 18-cm (7-inch) sandwich cake tins. Cream the fat and sugar until pale and fluffy. Beat the eggs in a little at a time, beating well after each addition ■ Lightly fold in half the flour, using a tablespoon, then fold in the rest ■ Place half the mixture in each tin and level it with a knife ■ Bake both cakes on the same shelf, at 190°C (375°F) mark 5, for about 20 minutes, or until they are well risen, golden, firm to the touch and beginning to shrink away from the sides of the tins. Turn out on to a wire rack. When cool, sandwich with jam and sprinkle the top with caster sugar.

Beating in eggs

Placing mixture in tins

VARIATIONS

This mixture may be varied in many ways.

Chocolate   Replace 45 ml (3 level tbsp) flour with 45 ml (3 level tbsp) cocoa powder. Sandwich the cakes together with vanilla or chocolate butter cream (see page 118).

Orange or Lemon   Add 10 ml (2 level tsp) grated orange or lemon rind to the mixture. Sandwich the cakes together with orange or lemon curd or orange or lemon butter cream. Use the juice of the fruit to make glacé icing for the top (see page 119).

Coffee   Add 10 ml (2 tsp) instant coffee powder or 15 ml (1 tbsp) strong black coffee to the creamed mixture, adding it with the egg.

LEMON SWISS ROLL

3 eggs, size 2
100 g (4 oz) caster sugar
100 g (4 oz) plain flour

150 ml (5 fl oz) double cream
about 275 g (10 oz) lemon curd

Grease a 33 × 23 × 1.5-cm (13 × 9 × ½-inch) Swiss roll tin. Line the base with greased greaseproof paper. Dust with caster sugar and flour ■ Whisk the eggs and sugar in a bowl until thick enough to leave a trail on the surface when the whisk is lifted. Sift in the flour and fold gently through the mixture ■ Turn the mixture into the prepared tin and level the surface. Bake in the oven at 200°C (400°F) mark 6 for 10–12 minutes or until the cake springs back when pressed lightly with a finger and

Trimming edges of cake

Making cut at untrimmed end

Rolling sponge

has shrunk away a little from the tin ■ Sugar a sheet of greaseproof paper and turn the cake out on to it. Roll up with the paper inside. Transfer to a wire rack and leave to cool for 30 minutes ■ Whip the cream until it just holds its shape. Unroll the Swiss roll and spread with three quarters of the lemon curd. Top with cream then roll up again and place on a serving plate.

CHERRY CAKE

175 g (6 oz) butter or
   margarine
175 g (6 oz) caster sugar
2 eggs, beaten
225 g (8 oz) self-raising
   flour

a pinch of salt
100–175 g (4–6 oz) glacé
   cherries, rinsed, well
   dried and quartered
vanilla flavouring
milk if required

Grease a loaf tin measuring about 23 × 12.5 cm (9 × 5 inches) and line with greased greaseproof paper ■ Cream the butter and sugar, then gradually beat in the eggs. Sift together the flour and salt and add the cherries ■ Fold this mixture into the creamed mixture and add a few drops of flavouring and enough milk to give a dropping consistency ■ Put into the prepared tin and bake in the oven at 180°C (350°F) mark 4 for 1¼–1½ hours, until firm to touch and golden in colour.

CHOCOLATE CAKE

75 g (3 oz) self-raising
  flour
30 ml (2 level tbsp)
  ground rice
100 g (4 oz) plain
  chocolate, grated
100 g (4 oz) butter or
  margarine
75 g (3 oz) caster sugar

5–10 ml (1–2 tsp) vanilla
  flavouring
2 eggs, beaten
chocolate butter cream
  (see page 118)
chocolate glacé icing (see
  page 119)
crystallised violets

Grease and line with greased greaseproof paper a
15-cm (6-inch) cake tin ■ Mix the flour and ground
rice. Put the grated chocolate into a small basin,
place over a saucepan of hot water and heat gently to
melt the chocolate ■ Cream the fat, sugar and
flavouring until pale and fluffy. Add the melted chocolate (which should be only just warm) to the creamed
mixture and mix lightly together ■ Beat in the
eggs a little at a time. Fold in the flour, put into the
tin and bake in the oven at 180°C (350°F) mark 4 for
1–1¼ hours ■ Turn out on to a wire rack to cool
■ When cold, split in half and fill with chocolate butter cream ■ Ice with glacé icing and decorate with
crystallised violets.

GINGERBREAD

225 g (8 oz) plain flour
10–15 ml (2–3 level tsp)
  ground ginger
10 ml (2 level tsp) baking
  powder
2.5 ml (½ level tsp)
  bicarbonate of soda
2.5 ml (½ level tsp) salt
90 ml (6 tbsp) syrup

15 ml (1 tbsp) black
  treacle (optional)
75 g (3 oz) butter or
  margarine
100 g (4 oz) soft brown
  sugar
1 egg, beaten
60–150 ml (2–5 fl oz)
  milk

Grease and line a 20.5-cm (8-inch) square tin with
greased greaseproof paper ■ Sift the dry ingredients together. Warm the syrup, treacle (if used),
fat and sugar. Make a well in the centre of the dry
ingredients and add the syrup mixture. Add the egg
and some of the milk, and stir well; add more milk if
necessary to give a pouring consistency ■ Pour
the mixture into the tin and bake in the oven at
170°C (325°F) mark 3 for about 1 hour, until firm to
the touch ■ Cool on a wire rack, remove the
paper and cut into squares.

CHRISTMAS CAKE

175 g (6 oz) glacé cherries	225 g (8 oz) seedless raisins
100 g (4 oz) candied peel	grated rind of ½ a lemon
275 g (10 oz) plain flour	275 g (10 oz) butter or
a pinch of salt	margarine
2.5 ml (½ level tsp)	275 g (10 oz) soft brown
ground cinnamon	sugar
2.5 ml (½ level tsp)	15 ml (1 tbsp) black
ground mixed spice	treacle
500 g (1 lb 2 oz) currants	6 eggs, beaten
225 g (8 oz) sultanas	45 ml (3 tbsp) brandy

Grease and line a 23-cm (9-inch) cake tin and tie a band of brown paper round the outside ■ Halve the cherries and chop the peel. Sift together the flour, salt and spices, add the fruit, mixing well, then add the lemon rind ■ Cream the butter and sugar until light and fluffy. Add the black treacle to the eggs and beat this mixture gradually into the creamed mixture ■ Fold in the flour and fruit, then the brandy ■ Bake in the oven at 150°C (300°F) mark 2 for about 4½ hours. To avoid over-browning, cover the top with several thicknesses of paper after 2½ hours. ■ For a richer flavour, prick the cooked cake with a fine skewer and slowly pour 30–45 ml (2–3 tbsp) brandy over it before storing ■ Store it wrapped in greaseproof paper in an airtight tin; or wrap the cake lightly in foil ■ Cover with almond paste and ready-to-roll fondant or royal icing (see pages 120–122) and decorate.

Tying paper round tin

Adding egg/treacle mixture

Folding in flour, fruit, brandy

Pouring brandy over cake

FRUIT CAKE

100 g (4 oz) butter or
  margarine
225 g (8 oz) self-raising
  flour
a pinch of salt
100 g (4 oz) sugar

50 g (2 oz) currants
50 g (2 oz) sultanas
30 ml (2 tbsp) chopped
  candied peel
2 eggs, beaten
about 60 ml (4 tbsp) milk

Grease and line with greased greaseproof paper an
18-cm (7-inch) cake tin ▪ Rub the fat into the flour
and salt until the mixture resembles fine breadcrumbs. Stir in the sugar, fruit and peel. Make a well
in the centre, pour in the egg and some of
the milk and gradually work in the dry ingredients,
adding more milk if necessary to give a dropping consistency ▪ Put the mixture into the tin and
level the top. Bake in the oven at 180°C (350°F)
mark 4 for about 1 hour, until the cake is golden
brown and firm to the touch ▪ Turn out and cool
on a wire rack.

APPLE CAKE

225 g (8 oz) self-raising
  flour
2.5 ml (½ level tsp)
  ground cinnamon
100 g (4 oz) butter or
  margarine
100 g (4 oz) soft brown
  sugar

2 eggs, beaten
50 g (2 oz) seedless
  raisins
2 cooking apples, stewed
  and pulped

Grease and line with greased greaseproof paper a
loaf tin measuring about 23 × 12.5 cm (9 × 5 inches) ▪
Sift together the flour and cinnamon. Cream together
the fat and sugar until light and fluffy. Gradually add
the beaten eggs. Fold in half the sifted flour. Add the
raisins and apple pulp and the remaining flour and
fold in ▪ Turn the mixture into the prepared tin
and bake in the oven at 170°C (325°F) mark 3 for
about 1½ hours ▪ Turn out, cool and serve cut in
slices and buttered.

SYRUP FLAPJACKS

Makes 8

50 g (2 oz) butter or
  margarine
50 g (2 oz) demerara
  sugar

100 g (4 oz) golden syrup
100 g (4 oz) rolled oats

Grease a 19-cm (7½-inch) square sandwich tin ▪
Place the butter, sugar and syrup in a saucepan and
heat gently, stirring, until melted. Add the rolled
oats and stir well ▪ Press the mixture into the tin
and bake in the oven at 180°C (350°F) mark 4 for
about 20 minutes until brown ▪ When it is firm,
cut into pieces, but leave to cool completely before
removing from the tin.

Melting butter, sugar, syrup

Adding rolled oats

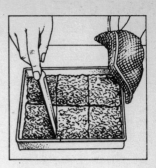

Cutting into pieces

CHOCOLATE CHIP COOKIES

Makes 20

75 g (3 oz) butter or margarine
75 g (3 oz) granulated sugar
75 g (3 oz) soft brown sugar
a few drops of vanilla flavouring

l egg
175 g (6 oz) self-raising flour
a pinch of salt
50 g (2 oz) walnuts, chopped
50–100 g (2–4 oz) chocolate chips

Grease 2 baking sheets ■ Cream the butter with the sugars and flavouring then beat in the egg. Fold in the sifted flour and salt, with the nuts and chocolate chips ■ Drop spoonfuls of mixture on the baking sheets and bake in the oven at 180°C (350°F) mark 4 for 12–15 minutes ■ Cool on the baking sheets for 1 minute, then place on a wire rack to finish cooling.

SHORTBREAD

Makes 8

Crimping edges

175 g (6 oz) plain flour
a pinch of salt

125 g (4 oz) butter
50 g (2 oz) caster sugar

Grease a baking sheet ■ Sift the flour and salt together, then rub in the butter until the mixture resembles fine breadcrumbs. Add the sugar, then knead the mixture until it binds well together ■ Turn this dough on to a lightly floured board and press into a round shape. Roll out to 1 cm (½ inch) thick, still keeping the round shape. Crimp the edges with the finger and thumb, mark the round into 8 sections with a knife and prick the surface with a fork ■ Bake in the oven at 170°C (325°F) mark 3 for about 45 minutes, until firm and lightly coloured. Divide when cool.

GINGERBREAD MEN

Makes 6

175 g (6 oz) plain flour
2.5 ml (½ level tsp) bicarbonate of soda
5 ml (1 level tsp) ground ginger
50 g (2 oz) butter or margarine

75 g (3 oz) soft brown sugar
30 ml (2 tbsp) golden syrup
30 ml (2 tbsp) beaten egg
currants to decorate

Grease a baking sheet ■ Sift together the dry ingredients and rub in the fat. Add the sugar and mix well ■ Stir in the slightly warmed syrup and egg to give a pliable dough, and knead until smooth ■ Roll out on a floured surface to a 3-mm (⅛-inch) thickness. Cut out, using a special cutter if available, or a cardboard template and a sharp-pointed knife. Carefully lift the gingerbread men on to the baking sheet, keeping them well apart ■ Give each one 3 currants for buttons and 3 more for eyes and mouth ■ Bake in the oven at 190°C (375°F) mark 5 for 10–15 minutes, until evenly coloured. Allow to cool before removing to a wire rack.

Cutting out gingerbread men

Decorating with currants

ONE-STAGE CAKES AND PASTRY

SANDWICH CAKE

100 g (4 oz) self-raising flour
5 ml (1 level tsp) baking powder
100 g (4 oz) soft tub margarine

100 g (4 oz) caster sugar
2 eggs
jam or lemon curd to fill

Grease two 18-cm (7-inch) sandwich tins and line each base with a round of greased greaseproof paper ■ Sift the flour and baking powder into a large bowl. Add the other ingredients, mix well, then beat for about 2 minutes. Divide evenly between the tins ■ Bake in the oven at 180°C (350°F) mark 4 for 25–35 minutes. When cool, sandwich with jam or lemon curd ■ For a more lavish decoration, sandwich together with butter cream and pour chocolate icing (see pages 118–119) over the top, letting it trickle down the sides.

VARIATIONS

Orange Add the grated rind and juice of 1 orange.

Mocha Sift 30 ml (2 level tbsp) cocoa and 15 ml (1 level tbsp) instant coffee powder with 75 g (3 oz) flour.

Chocolate, Cherry and Nut Cake Omit 30 ml (2 level tbsp) sugar and add 25 g (1 oz) grated plain chocolate, 75 g (3 oz) chopped glacé cherries and 60 ml (4 level tbsp) chopped nuts.

Small buns Make into 18–20 buns and bake in the oven at 200°C (400°F) mark 6 for 15–20 minutes.

FRUIT CAKE

225 g (8 oz) self-raising
  flour
10 ml (2 level tsp) ground
  mixed spice
5 ml (1 level tsp) baking
  powder
100 g (4 oz) soft tub
  margarine

100 g (4 oz) soft brown
  sugar
225 g (8 oz) dried fruit
2 eggs
30–45 ml (2–3 tbsp) milk

Grease an 18-cm (7-inch) round cake tin and line the base with a round of greased greaseproof paper ■ Sift the flour, spice and baking powder into a large bowl, add the rest of the ingredients and mix until thoroughly combined ■ Put into the tin and bake in the oven at 170°C (325°F) mark 3 for 1¾ hours.

CHOCOLATE CAKE

175 g (6 oz) self-raising
  flour
2.5 ml (½ level tsp)
  cream of tartar
2.5 ml (½ level tsp) salt
100 g (4 oz) sugar
100 g (4 oz) soft tub
  margarine or blended
  white vegetable fat

150 ml (¼ pint) milk
5 ml (1 tsp) vanilla
  flavouring
2 eggs
50 g (2 oz) plain
  chocolate, melted

Grease an 18-cm (7-inch) round cake tin ■ Sift the flour, cream of tartar and salt into a large bowl. Add the sugar, fat, milk and vanilla flavouring. Mix together then beat for 2 minutes ■ Add the eggs and chocolate and beat for 1 minute ■ Pour into the tin and bake in the oven at 180°C (350°F) mark 4 for about 1 hour 20 minutes.

TOFFEE BARS

Makes 8

100 g (4 oz) soft tub
  margarine or blended
  white vegetable fat
50 g (2 oz) sugar
50 g (2 oz) brown sugar
1.25 ml ('/4 level tsp) salt
5 ml (I tsp) vanilla
  flavouring

I egg
100 g (4 oz) self-raising
  flour
105 ml (7 tbsp) rolled oats
50 g (2 oz) plain ·
  chocolate
50 g (2 oz) chopped nuts

Grease a 23-cm (9-inch) shallow square tin ■ Mix
the fat, sugars, salt, flavouring and egg together until
light and fluffy. Stir in the flour and the oats ■
Spread the mixture in the tin and bake in the oven at
180°C (350°F) mark 4 for 30 minutes ■ Melt the
chocolate, spread on the cooled cake and sprinkle
with nuts ■ Cut into bars.

SHORTCRUST PASTRY

100 g (4 oz) soft tub
  margarine
175 g (6 oz) plain flour,
  sifted

about 15 ml (I tbsp)
  water

Place the margarine, 30 ml (2 tbsp) flour and the water
in a mixing bowl. Cream it with a fork for about
½ minute until well mixed ■ Mix in the remaining
flour, to form a fairly soft dough ■ Turn it out on
to a lightly floured board and knead until smooth.
Roll out fairly thinly ■ This amount is enough to
line a 20.5-cm (8-inch) fluted flan ring.

WHAT WENT WRONG?

RUBBED-IN AND CREAMED MIXTURES

A A cake that sinks in the middle may be due to

1 Too soft a mixture.
2 Too much raising agent.
3 Too cool an oven, which means that the centre
  of the cake does not rise.
4 Too hot an oven, which makes the cake appear
  to be done on the outside before it is cooked,
  so that it is taken from the oven too soon.
5 Too short a baking time.

B Close texture may be due to

1 Too much liquid
2 Too little baking powder
3 Insufficient creaming of the fat and sugar; air
  should be well incorporated at this stage.
4 Curdling of the creamed mixture when the eggs
  are added (a curdled mixture holds less air than
  one of the correct texture).
5 Over-stirring or beating of the flour into the
  creamed mixture.

C Uneven and holey texture may be caused by

1 Over-stirring or uneven mixing in of the flour.
2 Putting the mixture into the cake tin in small amounts – pockets of air are trapped in the mixture.

D Dry and crumbly texture may be due to

1 Too much baking powder.
2 Too long a cooking time in too cool an oven.

E 'Peaking' and cracking may be caused by

1 Too hot an oven.
2 The cake being placed too near the top of the oven.
3 Too stiff a mixture
4 Too small a cake tin.

F Fruit sinking in a cake may be due to

1 Damp fruit, or sticky glacé cherries – if covered with thick syrup they should first be washed, then lightly floured.
2 Too soft a mixture – a rich fruit cake mixture should be fairly stiff, so that it can hold up the weight of the fruit.
3 Opening and banging the oven door while the cake is rising.
4 Using self-raising flour where the recipe requires plain, or using too much baking powder; the cake over-rises and cannot carry the fruit with it.

G Dry fruit cakes may be due to

1 Cooking at too high a temperature.
2 Too stiff a mixture.
3 Not lining the tin thoroughly; for a large cake double greaseproof paper should be used, and a band of double brown paper should be tied round the outside of the tin to give extra protection.

H Burnt fruit on the outside of a fruit cake may be caused by

1 Too high a temperature.
2 Lack of protection – when the cake has begun to colour, cover the top with a double thickness of greaseproof or brown paper.

ICING AND DECORATING

BUTTER CREAM

100 g (4 oz) icing sugar
50 g (2 oz) butter or
  margarine

milk if required
a few drops of vanilla
  flavouring

Sift the sugar; place it with the butter in a basin and cream together with a wooden spoon until smooth, pale and of a creamy consistency – add a little milk if necessary. Beat in the vanilla flavouring ■ Or omit the vanilla flavouring and flavour the cream in any of the following ways:

Chocolate Include 15 ml (1 level tbsp) sifted cocoa or 25 g (1 oz) melted and cooled chocolate.

Coffee Add 10 ml (2 level tsp) instant coffee dissolved in 5 ml (1 tsp) water.

Mocha Add 10–15 ml (2–3 tsp) sifted cocoa and 5 ml (1 tsp) instant coffee powder.

Orange or lemon Add the grated rind of 1 orange or lemon.

Walnut Add 25–50 g (1–2 oz) chopped walnuts and a little vanilla flavouring.

USING BUTTER CREAM

The amounts given make enough cream for one layer inside or on top of the cake. If the cake is to be both decorated all over and filled with butter cream, you will require double the quantity.

AS A FILLING

Spread the cream evenly over the lower half of the cake, taking it right to the edges, then put the top half of the cake neatly in place.

TO COVER THE CAKE

Spread the butter cream evenly all over the sides, then on the top of the cake. The sides may be rolled in chopped nuts or chocolate vermicelli. To give a more interesting effect, the surface of the butter cream can be patterned, using a fork or knife, before being decorated with crystallised fruits, nuts, glacé cherries, angelica or chocolate drops.
Another variation is to coat the sides only with butter cream and use glacé icing on the top of the cake.

GLACÉ ICING

225 g (8 oz) icing sugar,   warm water to mix
  sifted

Adding water gradually

Place the sugar in a basin and add the water very gradually until the icing is smooth and thick enough to coat the back of the spoon.

This basic icing may be varied as follows:

Orange or lemon   Replace the water by orange or lemon juice.

Chocolate   Sift 15 ml (1 level tbsp) cocoa with the icing sugar.

Coffee   Dissolve 10 ml (2 level tsp) instant coffee in 5 ml (1 tsp) of the water and add this when mixing the icing.

Coloured   Use food colourings to tint the icing – only a few drops are needed and they should be added when the icing is made.

USING GLACÉ ICING

The amounts given will make enough icing to cover the top of an 18-cm (7-inch) cake. The sides of the cake may be left plain or iced (in which case you will need a double quantity of icing). Alternatively, they may be brushed with melted jam and then rolled in chopped walnuts, chopped blanched almonds or lightly browned coconut. Any icing or decoration on the sides of the cake must be done before the top is iced.

To ice the top, prepare any decorations which are to be used (such as nuts, cherries, angelica, chocolate drops, crystallised fruit, silver balls or candies). Place the prepared cake on the plate on which it is to be served. Pour the icing on to the centre of the cake and spread it out evenly, stopping just inside the edges to prevent the icing from dripping down the sides. Quickly put the decorations in place before the icing sets – this holds them firmly and prevents the icing from cracking as it would do if they were added later.

Rolling cake in chopped nuts

Spreading icing evenly

ROYAL ICING

4 egg whites (or albumen
    powder equivalent)
900 g (2 lb) icing sugar,
    sifted

15 ml (1 tbsp) lemon
    juice
10 ml (2 tsp) glycerine

Whisk the egg whites in a bowl until slightly frothy. Stir in the sugar, a spoonful at a time with a wooden spoon. When half the sugar is incorporated, add the lemon juice ■ Continue adding more sugar, beating well after each addition until you get the right consistency — the mixture should not peak when pulled up with a wooden spoon, it should be a little stiffer for piping purposes, and thinner for flooding — Lastly, stir in the glycerine, which helps prevent the icing from becoming too hard ■ If you use an electric mixer, take care not to overbeat. It is a good idea to let it stand for 24 hours in a covered plastic container or bag before using ■ This amount is sufficient to coat the top and sides of a 23-cm (9-inch) cake. To ice the top only, use half the quantities.

TO ICE THE CAKE

Using a little icing, stick the cake firmly in the centre of a 28-cm (11-inch) cake board ■ Spoon half the icing on top of the cake; working the icing backwards and forwards with a knife to break any air bubbles, spread it over the top of the cake. Draw a clean ruler or a long palette knife across the top of the cake evenly and steadily, until the surface is smooth ■ Remove any extra icing that has been pushed to the edges. Work the rest of the icing around the sides of the cake in the same way ■ Before the icing starts to set, quickly draw it up into peaks round the sides and in a 2.5-cm (1-inch) border round the top of the cake, using a round-bladed knife. Let the icing harden for a day before adding decorations ■ If you are icing the top only, take the icing far enough down the sides to cover the almond icing completely. Rough up a 3-cm (1¼-inch) wide border round the top and the covered part of the sides ■ When the icing is set, tie a ribbon round the sides.

Putting top on cake

Smoothing the join

ALMOND PASTE

350 g (12 oz) icing sugar
350 g (12 oz) ground almonds
1 egg, beaten

5 ml (1 tsp) almond flavouring
juice of ½ a lemon

Sift the sugar and stir in the almonds. Add the beaten egg and almond flavouring and gradually stir in the dry ingredients, adding enough of the lemon juice to form a stiff dough. Form into a ball and knead lightly to remove any cracks ■ This amount is sufficient to cover the top and sides of a 23-cm (9-inch) cake. If you intend to decorate the top only of the cake, make up half the amount. Cut off and reserve a small piece if you want to make almond paste decorations.

> If you wish to avoid using raw egg, mix the almond flavouring and lemon juice with a little water instead.

TO ALMOND-ICE THE CAKE

Trim the top of the cake to make it completely level. Measure round it, using a piece of string ■ Sieve 225 g (8 oz) apricot jam and brush it generously round the sides of the cake ■ Cut the almond paste in half. Halve one portion again and form each quarter-portion into a sausage-shape; roll out each of these half as long as the piece of string and as wide as the cake is deep ■ Press the strips firmly on to the sides of the cake, smooth the joins with a knife and square the edges ■ Roll the cake edgewise on the table or board to get a flat finish ■ Brush the top of the cake and the top edge of the almond paste with jam ■ Dredge the table top or board heavily with icing sugar, then roll out the remaining paste to a round to fit the top of the cake ■ Put the cake upside-down, exactly in the centre of the almond paste, press down firmly and smooth the join ■
Turn the cake the right way up and leave for at least 24 hours before icing – preferably for 6–7 days.

Smoothing icing

Smoothing icing on side

Squaring edges

ALMOND PASTE DECORATIONS

Decorations for a Christmas cake can be made very easily from almond paste. Choose a design with a simple, fairly bold outline – stars, candles, Christmas trees, holly leaves – draw it on stiff paper and cut out the template. Some parts of the design may look more attractive if carried out in a second colour, eg the tub of a Christmas tree or the flame of a candle, but do not use more than two colours, or the design will look too fussy. Cut off the portion of the paper template that is to be made in the second colour.

Add a little edible colouring to a piece of the almond paste, kneading it in until the colour is even. Sprinkle the working surface with a little icing sugar and roll out the almond paste very thinly. Put on it the templates that are to be made in that particular colour and cut round them with a sharp-pointed knife. (Do not press too firmly on the almond paste or finger marks will show.) Remove the templates, neaten up the edges of the paste pieces if necessary and use the pointed knife to mark in any veins, branches, etc. Cut out the remaining shapes from a piece of almond paste tinted with the second colour. For holly berries make tiny balls of red paste. Leave the shapes on a plate until quite dry – 2–3 days if possible – or they will mark the royal icing. Lay any leaves over a twist of greaseproof paper to give them a lifelike curve.

Draw a circle on a piece of paper the size of the cake top and arrange the almond paste pieces on it in the chosen pattern. Then, using a pair of tweezers, lift each piece into the same position on the cake top and stick it with a tiny spot of icing. A birthday cake may be decorated in a similar way; for a child, use nursery rhyme or toy cut-outs.

FONDANT ICING

Ready-made fondant or ready-to-roll icing is a convenient, easy-to-apply covering for cakes and is widely available. It is also called sugar paste, fondant paste or moulding icing, and can be cut, coloured, rolled, and shaped to make flowers and decorations.

BREADS AND SCONES

QUICK ROLLS

Makes 9

225 g (8 oz) plain flour
10 ml (2 level tsp) baking
  powder
5 ml (1 level tsp) salt

25 g (1 oz) butter or
  margarine
about 150 ml (¼ pint)
  milk

Sieve the dry ingredients into a bowl. Rub in the fat until the mixture resembles breadcrumbs ■ Make a well in the centre, add the milk and mix together with a round-bladed knife to a soft dough ■ Draw it together with fingertips and turn on to a lightly floured board ■ Divide into 9 portions and shape into rolls. Place on a greased and floured baking sheet, brush with milk and bake at 220°C (425°F) mark 7 for 15–20 minutes.

QUICK WHITE LOAF

Makes 2

15 g (½ oz) fresh yeast
  or 7.5 ml (1½ level tsp)
  dried yeast and a pinch
  of sugar

300 ml (½ pint) tepid water
450 g (1 lb) strong plain
  flour
5 ml (1 level tsp) salt

Grease 2 baking sheets ■ If using dried yeast, dissolve the sugar in the water, sprinkle in the yeast and leave for 10–15 minutes until frothy ■ Mix the flour and salt in a bowl, make a well in the centre and add the yeast liquid. Mix to an elastic dough, adding more liquid if necessary. Turn on to a lightly floured surface and knead for about 5 minutes, until really smooth. Divide the dough into 2 portions then knead each into a round ■ Place on a baking sheet and cover with a clean tea towel. Leave to rise in a warm place for about 30–45 minutes until it has doubled in size and will spring back when lightly pressed ■ Bake at 230°C (450°F) mark 8 for about 30 minutes until well risen and golden and sounding hollow when the bottom is tapped. Cool on a wire rack.

FAST ACTION YEAST

Also known as 'easy-blend yeast' and 'easy-mix yeast', this product has revolutionised bread-making. Fast-action yeast is simply mixed directly into the flour. After kneading, the dough can be shaped straight away and requires only one rising.
The recipes here give equivalents for fresh and dried yeast. If you use fast-action yeast you will need 1 sachet or 7.5 ml (1½ level tsp) to each 700 g (1½ lb) strong flour.

QUICK WHOLEMEAL LOAVES

Makes 2

15 ml (3 level tsp) sugar
about 450 ml (¾ pint) water
15 ml (1 level tbsp) dried yeast

350 g (12 oz) wholemeal flour
350 g (12 oz) strong white flour
15 ml (3 level tsp) salt

Grease 2 baking sheets ■ Dissolve 5 ml (1 tsp) sugar in a cupful of warm water (taken from the measured amount), then sprinkle the dried yeast on the top; leave until frothy (10–15 minutes) ■ Add with the rest of the liquid to the dry ingredients and mix to a soft, scone-like dough. Divide the dough into 2 portions, shape into rounds and flatten the tops ■ Place on a baking sheet, and cover with a clean dry tea towel. Leave to rise in a warm place until the dough is doubled in size and will spring back when lightly pressed with a floured finger ■ Bake in the oven at 220°C (425°F) mark 7 for about 30 minutes, or until the loaves are firm to the touch and sound hollow when tapped underneath.

Adding yeast to flour

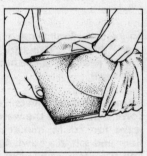
Covering dough

Loaves sliced

OVEN SCONES

Makes 10–12

225 g (8 oz) self-raising flour
1.25 ml (¼ level tsp) salt
50 g (2 oz) butter or margarine

25 g (1 oz) sugar
50 g (2 oz) currants
about 150 ml (¼ pint) milk

Stirring in sugar and currants

Rolling out dough

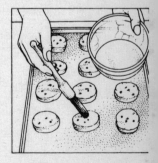
Brushing tops with milk

Grease a baking sheet ■ Sift the flour and salt into a bowl. Cut the fat into it and rub in until the mixture resembles fine breadcrumbs ■ Stir in the sugar and currants. Add the milk to give a fairly soft dough. Draw the mixture together with the finger-tips and turn on to a very lightly floured board; form into a flat round and roll out to a 2.5-cm (1-inch) thickness ■ Cut into rounds with a 5-cm (2-inch) cutter and place on the greased baking sheet. Brush the tops with milk and cook in the oven at 220°C (425°F) mark 7 for about 10 minutes until golden brown ■ Remove to a cooling rack and leave till cold ■ Serve split in half and buttered.

DROP SCONES OR SCOTCH PANCAKES

Makes 15–18

125 g (4 oz) self-raising flour
30 ml (2 level tbsp) sugar
1 egg
150 ml (¼ pint) milk

These scones may be cooked on a special griddle, in a heavy frying pan or on a solid hot-plate. Season the surface by rubbing with salt on a pad of kitchen paper; wipe clean and grease the surface very lightly ■ Put the flour and sugar in a bowl, break in the egg, add half the milk and beat until smooth. Add the rest of the milk and beat until bubbles rise to the surface ■ Heat the griddle, pan or hot-plate until the fat is hazing. Wipe the surface with a piece of kitchen paper, spoon on the batter and cook on one side ■ When bubbles appear on the surface of the scone, turn it over with a palette knife and cook for another ½–1 minute, or until golden brown ■ Remove and place on a wire rack. Cover with a clean tea cloth while the rest are being cooked ■ Serve buttered or with whipped cream and jam.

Spooning on the batter

Turning over pancakes

INDEX